Lotus
General Knowledge

Notes on aspects of fast developing modern world, especially information for competitive exams for interviews, etc.

• • •

Exhaustive and up-to-date

Published by :
Lotus Press Publishers & Distributors

Lotus
General Knowledge

Gaurav Shah

Lotus PRESS

4735/22, Prakash Deep Building,
Ansari Road, Darya Ganj
New Delhi-110002

Lotus Press Publishers & Distributors
Unit No. 220, 2nd Floor, 4735/22, Prakash Deep Building,
Ansari Road, Darya Ganj, New Delhi-110002
Ph.: 011-41325510, 98118-38000
•E-mail : lotuspress1984@gmail.com
www.lotuspress.co.in

Lotus General Knowledge

ISBN : 978-81-8382-341-8

Printed & Published by: **Lotus Press Publishers & Distributors,** New Delhi-02

PREFACE

The world around us is expanding fast as a result of globalization. The technology, on the other hand, is shrinking it. These factors have made it essential for every individual aspiring to make it big in any career-oriented field to have a good hold over knowledge pertaining to what has happened, what is happening, and what would happen. Such a knowledge base demands a sound foundation of not just the current issues affecting the world, but also a fine understanding of the events in the past and their effect on the present. The study of General Knowledge requires at least three processes: learning, that is acquiring knowledge; understanding of this knowledge; and memory retention.

The old system of structured presentation, and focus on highly predictable topics such as Indian government, geography, prizes and awards, United Nations, the state of Indian sports and medal- winning athletes, is on its way out. Fast replacing it is a far more heterogeneous mix that seeks to gauge the extent of knowledge that an examinee has accumulated over the entire span of his educational career. In fact, the new trend tests the depth and breadth of an examinee's personal knowledge bank.

The present book is a sure guide to success for candidates who are preparing to appear in various competitive exams that require them to have a sound understanding of the world around and a strong knowledge base of the events that occurred not just in India, but all around the world in the past centuries. The material of this book was collected on the type of questions asked. The book has been modeled so as to serve, as best as possible, the purpose of competitive examinations and to equip candidates with the basic general awareness required for their success in these examinations. A compilation of this nature could never have been attempted without reference to the works of others. In the preparation of this book I have had to constantly consult numerous encyclopedias, dictionaries, year books, atlases, and textbooks on a variety of subjects.

—Author

Other Books on

QUIZ & CAREERS

1. 100 Ways to Develop Self Confidence (New)
2. 100 Ways to Motivate Yourself (New)
3. How to Solve Math Puzzles
4. History Quiz Book
5. Lotus Mathematics Quiz Book
6. The Great Book of Riddles & Jokes
7. How to Improve Your IQ
8. Learn to Play Chess Tactics & Strategies
9. World's Greatest Puzzles
10. Brain Ticklers in Economics
11. Brain Ticklers in Mathematics
12. Brain Ticklers in Nature
13. Brain Ticklers in General Knowledge
14. Brain Ticklers in English
15. Quiz for All
16. Lotus General Knowledge
17. 1010 Riddles
18. Science Quiz
19. World Quiz
20. Facing Job Interviews
21. Preparing for Call Center Interviews
22. Sure Success in Interviews
23. Jokes for All

Contents

Common Abbreviations

1

A

AACI	Airport Association Council International
AAFI	Amateur Athletics Federation of India
AAGSP	All Assam Gana Sangam Parishad
AAPSO	Afro-Asian Peoples Solidarity Organization
AASU	All Assam Students Union
ABCDE	Annual Bank Conference on Development Economics
ABSU	All Bodo Students Union
ABT	Availability Based Tariff
AC	Alternate Current, or Ashok Chakra, or Air Conditioner, or Antarctic Club
AD	Anno Domini (After the birth of Jesus)
ADA	Air Defence Artillery
ADB	Asian Development Bank
AERE	Atomic Energy Research Establishment
AFLP	Accelerated Female Literacy
AFPPD	Asian Forum of Parliamentarians on Population & Development
AGF	Asian Games Federation
AGOC	Asian Games Organization Committee
AICC	All India Congress Committee
AICTE	All India Council of Technical Education
AICCTU	All India Central Council of Trade Unions
AICI	Agricultural Insurance Corporation of India
AIDS	Acquired Immune Deficiency Syndrome
AIDWA	All India Democratic Women's Association.
AIFF	All India Football Federation
AIIMS	All India Institute of Medical Sciences
AIMPLB	All India Muslim Personal Law Board

AINEC	All India Newspaper Editors' Conference
AIR	All India Radio
AITUC	All India Trade Union Congress
ALH	Advanced Light Helicopter
AMIE	Associate Member of the Institute of Engineers
ANC	African National Congress
APNN	Asian Pacific News Network
APEC	Asian Pacific Economic Cooperation
APEDAA	Agricultural and Processed Food Products Export Development Authority Act.
APPU	Asian Pacific Postal Union
ARF	Asian Regional Forum
ARDS	Acute Respiratory Distress Syndrome
ASEAN	Association of South East Asian Nations
ASI	Archaeological Survey of India
ASSOCHAM	Associated Chamber of Commerce and Industry (India)
AWACS	Airborne Warning and Control System
ATCI	Air Time Committee of India
ATF	Aviation Turbine Fuel
ATPLO	All Tripura Peoples Liberation Organization
ATS	Anti Tetanus Serum
AVARD	Association of Voluntary Agencies for Rural Development

ASI

B

BAMS	Bachelor of Ayurvedic Medicine and Surgery
BARC	Bhabha Atomic Research Centre
BBC	British Broadcasting Corporation
BCG	Bacillus Calmette Guerin (Anti TB Vaccine)
BCCI	Board of Control for Cricket in India
BCCL	Bharat Cooking Coal Limited
BENELUX	Belgium, Netherlands and Luxemburg
BFC	Business Facilitation Council.
BHEL	Bharat Heavy Electronics Limited
BICP	Bureau of Industrial Costs and Prices
BIFR	Board of Industrial Finance and Reconstruction
BIMSTEC	Bangladesh, India, Myanmar, Sri Lanka, Thailand Economic Cooperation

BIS	Bureau of Indian Standards/British Information Service/Bank for International Settlements
BLTF	Bodo Liberation Tigers Force
BPO	Business Process Outsourcing
B.PHARMA	Bachelor of Pharmacy
BRL	Bharat Refineries Ltd
BSF	Border Security Force
BTC	Bodoland Territorial Council

C

CAD	Command Area Development
CAG	Controller and Auditor General
CAIR	Centre for Artificial Intelligence and Robotics
CAS	Conditional Access System
CASE	Commission for Alternative Sources of Energy
CAT	Control for Advance Technology/Central Administrative Tribunal
CAZRI	Central Arid Zone Research Institute
CBDT	Central Board of Direct Taxes
CBEC	Central Board of Excise and Customs
CBI	Central Bureau of Investigation
CBSE	Central Board of Secondary Education
CCEA	Cabinet Committee on Economic Affairs
CCIC	Central Cottage Industries Corporation
CCIT	Comprehensive Convention on International Terrorism
CDC	Consulting Development Centre
CDRI	Central Drug Research Institute
CDS	Compulsory Deposit Scheme
CEA	Central Electrical Authority
CFRI	Central Fuel Research Institute
CFTRI	Central Food Technological Research Institute
CGWB	Central Ground Water Board
CHOGM	Commonwealth Heads of Government Meeting
CID	Criminal Investigation Department
CIFT	Committee on Invisible Financing Related Trade
CIMA	Centre of International Modern Art
CIRDAP	Council of Integrated Rural Development for Asia and the Pacific
CIRTES	Central Institute for Research and Training in Employment Services

CIS	Commonwealth of Independent States
CITU	Centre of Indian Trade Union
CIWTC	Central Inland Water Transport Corporation
CLASP	Child Labour Action and Support Project
CMAG	Commonwealth Ministerial Action Group
CMAL	Coal Mines Authority Limited
CMDRO	Central Marine Design Research Organization
CMPDI	Central Mine Planning and Design Institute
CNG	Compressed Natural Gas
COD	Central Ordinance Depot
CODESA	Convention for a Democratic South Africa
COFEPOSA	Conservation of Foreign Exchange and Prevention of Smuggling Act
COSPAR	Committee on Space Research
COPU	Committee on Public Undertaking (under Parliament)
CORE	Congress on Racial Equality
CPCB	Central Pollution Control Board
CPCRI	Central Plantation Crops Research Institute
CPO	Central Passport Organization
CPRI	Central Power Research Institute
CRP	Central Reserve Police
CRR	Cash Reserve Ratio
CSE	Centre for Science and Environment
CSCE	Conference on Security and Cooperation in Europe
CTEPC	Cotton Textiles Export Promotion Council
CTS	Computerised Tomography Scanner
COCA	Control of Organized Crime Act
CVC	Central Vigilance Commission

CNG

COSEPOSA

D

DAVP	Directorate of Advertising and Visual Publicity
DCA	Drug and Cosmetic Act
DCI	Dredging Corporation of India
DDT	Dichloro Diphenyle Trichloroethane
DDP	Desert Development Programme

DAVP

DFDR	Digital Flight Data Recorder (Black Box)
DIG	Deputy Inspector General
DGCA	Director General of Civil Aviation
DICGC	Deposit Insurance and Credit Guarantee Corporation
DLO	Dead Letter Office
DGCEI	Directorate General of Central Excise Intelligence
DM	District Magistrate
DMK	Dravida Munetra Kazhagam
DMRL	Defence Metallurgical Research Laboratory
DNA	Di-oxyribo Nucleic Acid
DNEM	Dynamic Numeric Encoding Method
DPAP	Drought prone Area Programme
DPCS	Defence Satellite Communication System
DPCO	Drug Prices Control Order
DPSA	Deep Penetration Strike Aircraft
DRDO	Defence Research and Development Organization
DRI	Director of Revenue Intelligence
DST	Department of Science & Technology
DTH	Direct To Home
DOTS	Directly Observed Treatment Shortcourse
DVC	Damodar Valley Corporation
DVD	Digital Versatile Disc

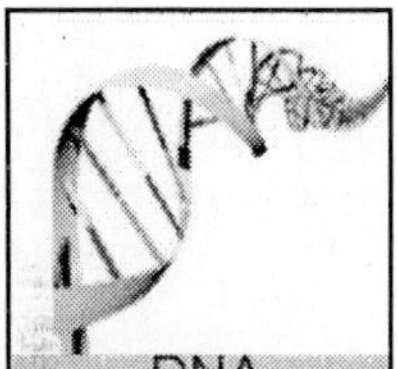
DNA

DOTS

E

EAA	Easy Animal Aid
EAS	Employment Assurance Scheme
ECB	European Central Bank
ECG	Electro-Cardiogram Graph
ECIL	Electronic Corporation of India Limited
EEC	European Economic Community
EEG	Electro-Encephalogram Graph
EFTA	European Free Trade Association
EGPWS	Enhanced Ground Proximity Warning System
EHTP	Electronics Hardware Technology Park
ELCINA	Electronics and Radar Development Establishment
EMF	Electromotive Force

EAA

EMF

EMI	Equal Monthly Installment
EMS	European Monetary System
EMU	Electric Multiple Unit
EOW	Economic Offence Wing
EPIP	Export Promotion Industrial Park
EPZ	Export Processing Zone
ERDA	Energy Research and Development Administration
ERS	European Remote Sensing Satellite
ERTS	Earth Resources Technology Satellite
ESA	European Space Agency
ESCAP	Economic and Social Commission for Asia and Pacific
EVM	Electronic Voting Machine
EVTR	Electro-Video Tape Recording
EXIM	Export-Import Bank of India
EURECA	European Research Coordinating Agency

F

FAO	Food and Agriculture Organization
FBI	Federal Bureau of Investigation
FBTR	Fast Breeder Test Reactor
FCV	Flue-Cured Virginia (a kind of tobacco)
FCI	Food Corporation of India/Fertilizer Corporation of India
FDR	Flight Data Recorder (Black Box)
FERA	Foreign Exchange Regulation Act
FEMA	Foreign Exchange Management Act
FFI	Film Federation of India
FICCI	Federation of Indian Chamber of Commerce and Industry
FIEO	Federation of Indian Export Organization
FIIT	Foundation for Innovation and Technology Transfer
FIPB	Foreign Investment Promotion Board
FRS	Fellow of the Royal Society
FTII	Films & Television Institute of India
FTZ	Free Trade Zone

G

GAIL	Gas Authority of India Limited
GATT	General Agreement on Tariff and Trade
GAVI	Global Alliance for Vaccine and Immunization
GIC	General Insurance Corporation
GMPCS	Global Mobile Personal Communications System
GMRT	Giant Meterweb Radio Telescope
GMT	Greenwich Mean Time
GNLF	Gorkha National Liberation Front
GNP	Gross National Product
GPF	General Provident Fund
GPO	General Post Office
GPRS	General Packet Radio Service
GPS	Global Positioning System
GRA	Global Research Alliance
GSD	Global Spatial Data Infrastructure
GSI	Geological Survey of India
GSLV	Geo Synchronous Satellite Launch Vehicle
GSOMIA	General Security of Military Information Agreement

H

HAC	Hindustan Aluminium Corporation
HADP	Hill Area Development Programme
HAL	Hindustan Aeronautics Limited
HARTRDN	Haryana State Electricity Development Corporation Limited
HCF	Highest Common Factor
HDFC	Housing Development Finance Corporation
HDTV	High Definition Television
HEC	Heavy Engineering Corporation
HEL	Heavy Electricals Limited
HISA	Hero Indian Sports Academy
HIV	Human Immunodeficiency Virus
HMI	Himalayan Mountaineering Institute
HMT	Hindustan Machine Tools
HPTS	High Power Television Transmitter System

HRC	Human Rights Commission
HRD	Human Resource Development
HTR	High Temperature Reactor
HUDCO	Housing and Urban Development Corporation

I

IAAI	International Airport Authority of India
IAC	Indian Airlines Corporation
IADF	International Agriculture Development Fund
IAEA	International Atomic Energy Agency
IAPPD	Indian Association of Parliamentarians on Population and Development
IARI	Indian Agricultural Research Institute
IATA	International Air Transport Association
IBRD	International Bank for Reconstruction and Development (World Bank)
IBWL	Indian Board of Wild Life
ICAC	International Council of Adult Education
ICAI	Institute of Chartered Accountants of India
ICAR	Indian Council of Agricultural Research
ICBM	Inter-Continental Ballistic Missile
ICC	International Cricket Council
ICCR	Indian Council of Cultural Relations
ICCW	Indian Council of Child Welfare
ICHR	Indian Council for Historical Research
ICICI	Industrial Credit and Investment Corporation of India Ltd.
ICJ	International Court of Justice
ICMR	Indian Council of Medical Research
ICO	Islamic Conference Organization
ICPA	Indian Cricket-Players Association
ICRC	International Committee of the Red Cross
ICRISAT	International Crops Research Institute for the Semi Arid Tropics
ICSI	Institute of Company Secretaries India
ICSSR	Indian Council of Social Science Research

ICWAI Institute of Costs and Works Accounts of India
IDA International Development Agency
IDBI Industrial Development Bank of India
IDO International Defence Organization
IDPL Indian Drugs and Pharmaceuticals Limited
IED Improvised Explosives Device
IFA Indian Football Association
IFAD International Fund for Agricultural Development
IFCI Industrial Finance Corporation of India
IFFI International Film Festival of India
IFFCO Indian Farmers Fertilizers Cooperative
IFFS International Federation of Film Societies
IGMCO Inter-Government Maritime Consultative Organization
IGNCA Indira Gandhi National Centre for Arts
IGNOU Indira Gandhi National Open University
IIAS Indian Institute of Advanced Studies
IIBM Indian Institute of Business Management
IIDR International Institute for Development Research
IIPA Indian Institute of Public Administration
IIS Indian Institute of Sciences
IISCO Indian Iron and Steel Company
IIT Indian Institute of Technology
ILO International Labour Organization
IMA Indian Military Academy
IMF Indian Mountaineering Foundation/ International Monetary Fund
INGCA Indira Gandhi Gallery for Culture and Art
INMURSA International Maritime Satellite Organization
INMAS Institute of Nuclear Medicine and Allied Sciences
INS Indian Naval Ship/Indian Newspapers Society
INSDOC Indian National Scientific Documentation Centre
INTAC Indian National Trust for Art and Culture
INTELSAT International Telecommunication Satellite

INTERPOL	Interpole Police Organization
INCOSPAR	Indian National Committee for Space Research
INTUC	Indian National Trade Union Congress
IOC	International Olympic Committee/ Indian Oil Corporation
IPCC	Inter-government Panel on Climate Change
IPI	International Press Institute
IPKF	Indian Peace-Keeping Force
IQ	Intelligence Quotient
IRA	Irish Republic Army/Insurance Regulatory Authority
IRAS	Infrared Astronomical Satellite
IRBM	Intermediate Range Ballistic Missile
IRCS	Indian Red Cross Society
IRDP	Integrated Rural Development Programme
IRO	International Refugee Organization
ISAF	International Security Assistance Force
ISAS	Institute of Space and Astronomical Science
ISBA	International Sea Bed Authority
ISCUS	Indo-Soviet Cultural Society
ISE	International Stock Exchange
ISM	Indian School of Mines
ISO	International Standardized Organization/Indian Space Organization
ISRO	Indian Space Research Organization
ISS	Institute of Social Sciences
ISSP	Indian Scientific Satellite Project
IST	Indian Standard Time
ITBP	Indo-Tibet Border Police
ITDC	Indian Tourism Development Corporation
ITPO	Indian Trade Promotion Organization
ITO	International Trade Organization
ITU	International Telecommunication Union
ITUC	Indian Trade Union Congress
IUCNNR	International Union for the Conservation of Natural and National Research

IVRS	Interactive Virus Response System
IWT	Indus Water Treaty

J

JCWI	Joint Council for the Welfare of Immigrants
JKLF	Jammu-Kashmir Liberation Front
JMM	Jharkhand Mukti Morcha
JNU	Jawaharlal Nehru University
JPC	Joint Parliamentery Committee

JMM

K

KARP	Kalpakkam Atomic Reprocessing Plant
KG	Kinder-Garten
KRM	Kashmir Resolution Movement
KSTPS	Kota Super Thermal Power Station
KVIC	Khadi and Village Industries Commission

L

LAHDC	Ladakh Hill Development Council
LASER	Light Amplification by Stimulated Emission of Radiation
LDC	Lower Division Clerk
LIC	Life Insurance Corporation of India
LLB	Bachelor of Law
LLD	Doctor of Law
LLM	Master of Law
LMG	Light Machine Gun
LOC	Line of Control
LPA	Laws Prevention Association of India
LSD	Lysergic Acid Di-ethylamide

LAHDC

LIC

M

MA	Master of Arts
MAIT	Manufacturers; Association of Information Technology
MAPP	Madras Atomic Power Project
MASER	Microwave Amplification by Stimulated Emission of Radiation
MBA	Master of Business Administration
MBBS	Bachelor of Medicine and Bachelor of Surgery

MCA	Master of Computer Application
MCC	Melbourne Cricket Club
MD	Doctor of Medicine
MECL	Mineral Exploration Corporation Limited
MEET	Mission for Extension of Educational Technology
MERC	Maharashtra Electricity Regulatory Commission
METO	Middle East Treaty Organization
MFALA	Marginal Farmers and Agricultural Labour Agency
MFALS	Marginal Farmers and Agricultural Liberation Scheme
MI	Military Intelligence
MIGA	Multilateral Investment Guarantee Agency
MIT	Massachusetts Institute of Technology
MLA	Member of Legislative Assembly
MLC	Member of Legislative Council
MMDS	Multiple Microwave Distribution System
MMTC	Minerals and Metals Trading Corporation
MNAMS	Member of National Academy of Medical Sciences
MRTPC	Monopoly and Restrictive Trade Practice Commission
MRTS	Mass Rapid Transport System
MSA	Maritime Safety Agency
MST	Multi System Transmission
MTCT	Mother to Child Transmission
MODVAT	Modified Value Added Tax

N

NABARD	National Bank for Agricultural and Rural Development
NACO	National AIDS Control Organization
NADAMS	National Agricultural Drought Assessment and Monitoring System
NAEP	National Adult Educational Programme
NAFTA	North American Free Trade Agreement

NAPP Narora Atomic Power Plant

NASA National Aeronautic and Space Administration

NASDAQ National Association of Security Dealers' Active Quotation

NASSCOM National Association of Software & Service Companies

NATO North Atlantic Treaty Organization

NBCC National Building and Construction Corporation

NBCW Nuclear, Biological, Chemical Warfare

NBPGR National Bureau of Plant Genetic Resources

NBTB National Biotechnology Board

NBER National Bureau of Economic Research

NCAER National Council for Applied Economic Research

NCB Narcotics Control Bureau

NCCF National Consumers Cooperative Federation

NCDA National Coal Development Authority

NCDC National Cooperative Development Corporation

NCERT National Council of Educational Research and Training

NCFSE National Curriculum Framework for Secondary Education

NCRA National Centre for Radio Astrophysics

NCRB National Crime Record Bureau

NCSTC National Council for Science and Technology Communication

NCW National Commission for Women

NDA National Defence Academy

NDDB National Dairy Development Board

NDF National Defence Fund

NDPDC National Drugs and Pharmaceutical Development Council

NEERI National Environment Engineering Research Institute

NEFA North East Frontier Agency

NEPA National Environment Protection Authority

NFDC National Film Development Corporation

NFIW — National Federation of Indian Women

NFL — National Fertilizer Limited

NHPC — National Hydroelectric Power Corporation

NHRC — National Human Rights Commission

NICD — National Institute of Communicable Diseases

NIDC — National Industrial Development Corporation

NIIT — National Institute of Information Technology

NIMHANS — National Institute of Mental Health and Neuro-Science

NITIE — National Institute for Training in Industrial Engineering

NMDC — National Mineral Development Corporation

NMDS — National Missile Defence System

NMEP — National Malaria Eradication Programme

NMHC — National Material Handling Council

NOAA — National Oceanic and Atmospheric Administration

NOIDA — New Okhla Industrial Development Authority

NPB — Nuclear Power Board

NPCC — National Project Construction Corporation

NPCIL — Nuclear Power Corporation of India Limited

NPL — National Physical Laboratory

NPP — National Population Policy

NRC — National Reconstruction Core

NRDC — National Research and Development Corporation

NREP — National Rural Employment Programme

NRI — Non Resident Indian

NSC — National Security Council / National Savings Certificate

NSCN — National Socialist Council of Nagaland

NSS — National Service Scheme

NSSTC — National Space Science and Technology Centre

NSTEDB — National Science and Technology Entrepreneurship Development Board

NTC — National Textile Corporation

NTPC	National Thermal Power Corporation

O

OAPNA	Organization of Asia and Pacific News Agency
OAU	Organization of African Unity
OECD	Organization for Economic Cooperation and Development
OGL	Open General License
OIL	Oil India Limited
ONGC	Oil and Natural Gas Commission
OMSS	Open Market Sale Scheme
OPEC	Organization of Petroleum Exporting Countries
OPPI	Organization of Pharmaceutical Producers of India
OSCE	Organization of European Security Council

P

PACS	Primary Agricultural Credit Society
PAFNA	Pan African News Agency
PATA	Pacific Asia Travel Association
PCI	Press Council of India
PCS	Provincial Civil Services
PEO	Programme Evaluation Organization
Ph.D.	Doctor of Philosophy
PIB	Press Information Bureau
PGIMR	Post Graduate Institute of Medical Research
PLO	Palestine Liberation Organization
PMSSY	Pradhan Mantri Swasthya Suraksha Yojna
PM	Post Meridian / Prime Minister
POTA	Prevention of Terrorism Act
PSLV	Polar Satellite Launch Vehicle
PTI	Press Trust of India
PTO	Please Turn Over
PTCT	Parents to Child Transmission
PUCC	Pollution Under Control Certificate
PUCL	Peoples' Union for Civil Liberties
PUDR	Peoples' Union for Democratic Rights
PVC	Poly Vinyl Chloride / Param Vir Chakra

PWD	Public Works Department
PWG	Peoples' War Group

R

RAPP	Rajasthan Atomic Power Project
R&D	Research and Development
RBI	Reserve Bank of India
RCC	Reinforced Cement Concrete
RDSO	Research Design and Standard Organization
RDX	Research Development Explosive
REACH	Rural Entrepreneurship for Art and Culture Heritage
RGNDWM	Rajiv Gandhi National Drinking Water Mission
RITES	Rail India Technical and Economic Services
RMS	Railway Mail Service
RPNNL	Rashtriya Pariyojana Nirman Nigam Limited
RLEGP	Rural Landless Employment Guarantee Programme
RNA	Ribonucleic Acid
ROSNI	Round Spermatic Nuclear Injection
RSS	Rashtriya Swayamsevak Sangh
RTRA	Rail Tariff Regulatory Authority

S

SAAF	South Asian Accountants Federation
SADCC	South African Development Corporation Conference
SAFMA	South Asian Free Media Association
SAHR	South Asians for Human Rights
SAI	Sports Authority of India
SAIL	Steel Authority of India Limited
SARS	Service Acute Respiratory Syndrome
SATO	South Atlantic Treaty Organization
SATTE	South Asian Travel and Tourism Exchange
SC	Security Council / Supreme Court / Scheduled Caste
SCHIL	Stock Holding Corporation of India

SCI Shipping Corporation of India
SCL Space Corporation Limited
SCOPE Standing Conference of Public Enterprises
SCRA Special Class Railway Apprentice
SDR Special Drawing Rights
SEATO South East Asia Treaty Organization
SEBI Security Exchange Board of India
SEEPZ Santacruz Electronic Export Processing Zone
SEO Satellite for Earth Observation
SERC Structural Engineering Research Centre

SEBI

SEWA Self Employed Women's Association
SFC Strategic Force Command
SGPC Shiromani Gurudwara Prabandhak Committee
SHAR Shri-Harikota Range
SAHMAT Safdar Hashmi Memorial Trust
SIAM Society of Indian Automobiles' Manufacturers
SIDS Sudden Infant Death Syndrome

SIDBI Small Industries Development Bank of India
SIS Secret Intelligence Service
SIV Semen Immunodeficiency Virus
SLAR Sight-Looking Environment Radar
SLBM Submarine Launch Ballistic Missile
SLV Satellite Launch Vehicle
SMART Small Mission for Advanced Research

SIAM

SMS Short Messaging System
SNIPES Society of National Institutes for Physical Education and Sports
SPCA Society for the Prevention of Cruelty to Animals
SSD Satellite System Division
SSTEP Symphonic Satellite Telecommunication Experiment Project
START Strategic Armed Reduction Talks

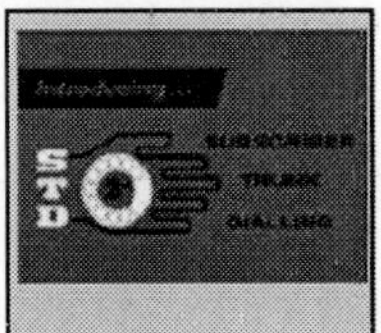
STD

STD	Subscribers-Trunk Dialing
STEC	Solar Thermal Energy Centre
STEP	Satellite Telecommunication Experiment Project
STPI	Software Technology Park of India
SUNFED	Special United Nations Fundfor Economic Development
SWAPO	South West African Peoples' Organization

T

TACDE	Tactics & Aircrafts Development Establishment
TAPS	Tarapur Atomic Power Station
TANSI	Tamil Nadu Small Industries Corporation
TAMP	Tariff Authority for Major Port's
TB	Tuberculosis
TCI	Trading Corporation of India
TCPO	Town and Country Planning Organization
TELCO	Tata Engineering and Locomotive Company
TELEX	Teleprinter Exchange
TERLS	Thumba Equatorial Rocket Launching Station
TIFAC	Technology Information Forecasting and Assessment Council
TISCO	Tata Iron & Steel Company
TIN	Taxpayer's Identification Number
TMO	Telegraphic Money Order
TNT	Tri Nitro Toluene
TRAI	Telecom Regulatory Authority of India
TRQ	Tariff Rate Quota
TTFI	Table Tennis Federation of India
TWA	Trans-World Airlines
TWAS	Third World Academy of Science
TWHS	Traditional Water Harvesting Systems
TWMF	Third World Monetary Fund
TWSI	Tourism and Wild Life Society of India

U

UANC

UANC United African National Council
UDC Upper Division Clerk /University Development Commission
UGC University Grant Commission
ULFA United Liberation Front of Assam
UNAEC United Nations Atomic Energy Commission
UNCED United Nations Conference on Environment and Development
UNCHS United Nations Commission on Human Settlements
UNCLOS United Nations Conference on Law of the Sea
UNCSTD United Nations Conference on Sciences and Technology for Development
UNCTC United Nations Counter-Terrorism Committee
UNCTAD United Nations Conference on Trade and Development
UNDP United Nations Development Programme
UNECAFE United Nations Economic Commission for Asia and Far East
UNEF United Nations Emergency Force
UNEP United Nations Environment Programme
UNESCO United Nations Economic and Social Commission
UNFPA United Nations Framework for Population Activities
UNHCR United Nations High Commission for Refugees

UNI United News of India
UNICEF United Nations International Children's Emergency Fund
UNIDO United Nations Industrial Development Organization
UNISPACE United Nations Conference on Exploration and Peaceful Usage of Outer Space
UNO United Nations Organization
UNRRA United Nations Relief and Rehabilitation Administration
UNSCOM United Nations Special Commission
UNTAG United Nations Transition Assistance Group
UPROV Union for Protection of New Varieties of Plants

UPSC

UPSC Union Public Service Commission
UPTN Universal Personal Tele Number

UPU Universal Postal Union
USAID United States Agency for International Development
USIS United States Information Service
USITC United States International Trade Corporation
USSR Union of Soviet Socialist Republic

V

VABAL Value Based Advanced License
VAT Value Added Tax
VIP Very Important Person
VPP Value Payable Post
VRDE Vehicle Research and Development Establishment
VRS Voluntary Retirement Scheme
VSNL Videsh Sanchar Nigam Limited
VSSC Vikram Sarabhai Space Centre

W

WANO World Association of Nuclear Operators
WAY World Assembly of Youth
WEF World Economic Forum
WFTU World Federation of Trade Union's
WHO World Health Organization
WIDF Women's International Democratic Federation
WIPO World Intellectual Property Organization
WIPSA Women's Initiative for Peace in South Asia
WWF World Wild Life Fund
WWPA World Wild Life Protection Agency

Y

YMCA Young Men's Christians Association
YWCA Young Women's Christians Association

Z

ZBB Zero Base Budgeting
ZIP Zone Improvement Plan
ZUPO Zimbabwe United People's Organization

❑❑❑

Recognized Days to Observe 2

January

- **January 1** — Global Family Day - formerly One Day of Peace and Sharing, recognized by the UN
- **January 1** — World Day of Peace - established by Pope Paul VI in his letter dated on 8.12.1967
- **January 6** — World Day for War Orphans - initiated by S.O.S Enfants En Detresse - by Stephen N. Kinuthia
- **January 11** — International Day for Peace in Kenya January 11, 2008. Recent events in the country left Kenyans in fear of their future. The stalmate between the political leaders has created opportunity for destructive forces, and organized militia, which have risen to kill innocent people (more than 450 killed, thousands injured and over 250,000 displaced - initiated by Kenya Welfare Foundation & Kenya Development Network and Consortium
- **January 15** — Army day
- **3rd Sunday of January** — World Religion Day - established in 1950
- **January 24** — National Girl Child Day of India, recognized by India
- **January 26** — Republic Day of India
- **January 27** — International Holocaust Remembrance Day, recognized by the UN
- **January 28** — Data Protection Day - recognized by the Council of Europe
- **January 29** — World Leprosy Day

- **January 30** — Martyrs Day of Mahatma Gandhi, Father of the Nation

February

- **February 4** — World Cancer Day
- **February 11** — World Day of the Sick, an observance day instituted by pope John Paul II.
- **February 12** — Darwin Day
- **February 14** — Valentines Day
- **February 20** — World Day of Social Justice, recognized by the UN
- **February 21** — International Mother Language Day, recognized by the UN World Tourist Guide
- **February 22** — International Scouts Day and World Thanking Day, for Girl Guides, Girl Scouts and Boy Scouts

March

- **March 4** — World Kamau's Day - Recognized by the UN
- **March 6** — Dentist's Day
- **March 8** — International Women's Day, recognized by the UN
- **March 14** — International Day of Action for Rivers
- **March 15** — World Day of Muslim Culture, Peace, Dialogue and Film

- **March 15** — World Consumer Rights Day
- **March 20** — World Day of Theatre for Children and Young People
- **March 21** — World Poetry Day, recognized by the UNESCO
- **March 22** — World Day for Water, recognized by the UN
- **March 23** — World Meteorological Day, recognized by the UN
- **March 24** — International Day for Achievers, World Tuberculosis Day, recognized by the UN

- **March 25** – International Day of Remembrance of the Victims of Slavery and the Transatlantic Slave Trade, recognized by the UN
- **March 27** – World Theatre Day

April

- **April 2** – World Autism Awareness Day, recognized by the UN
- **April 4** – International Day for Mine Awareness and Assistance in Mine Action, recognized by the UN
- **April 7** – World Health Day, recognized by the UN
- **April 14** – Cultural Unity Day, recognized by India, Sri Lanka, Maldives, Bangladesh and Nepal.

- **April 15** – Leonardo da Vinci's Birthday
- **April 16** – World Entrepreneurship Day (WED)
- **April 17** – World Hemophilia Day, recognized by the UN
- **April 21** – World Creativity and Innovation Day. Celebrations begin
- **April 22** – Earth Day
- **April 23** – World Book and Copyright Day, recognized by the UN

- **April 24** – World Day for Laboratory Animals, recognized by the UN
- **April 25** – World Malaria Day, recognized by the WHO
- **April 26** – World Intellectual Property Day, recognized by the UN
- **April 28** – International Workers' Memorial Day
- **April 29** – World Dance Day

May

- **May 1** – Labour Day
- **May 2** – International Day of the Deliberately Unemployed
- **May 3** – World Press Freedom Day, recognized by the UN

- **May 4** – International Firefighters' Day, Star Wars Day
- **May 5** – International Midwives Day
- **May 8** – World Red Cross & Red Crescent Day
- **May 12** – International Nurses Day
- **May 15** – International Day of Families, recognized by the UN
- **May 17** – World Information Society Day, recognized by the UN
- **May 18** – International Museum Day
- **May 19** – World Hepatitis Day
- **May 21** – World Day for Cultural Diversity for Dialogue and Development, recognized by the UN
- **May 22** – International Day for Biological Diversity, recognized by the UN
- **May 23** – World Turtle Day
- **May 29** – International Day of United Nations Peacekeepers, recognized by the UN
- **May 29** – Redhead Day in Walibi Belgium
- **May 31** – World No Tobacco Day, recognized by the UN
- **1st Tuesday of May** – World Asthma Day
- **2nd Saturday of May** – World Fair Trade Day
- **2nd Sunday of May** – International Mothers' Day

June

- **June 1** – International Children's Day

- **June 4** – International Day of Innocent Children Victims of Aggression, recognized by the UN
- **June 5** – World Environment Day, recognized by the UN
- **June 8** – World Brain Tumour Day
- **June 8** – World Ocean Day
- **June 10** – Ballpoint Pen Day
- **June 12** – World Day Against Child Labour
- **June 14** – World Blood Donor Day, recognized by the UN

- **June 18** — International Picnic Day
- **June 19** — World Sickle Cell Day, by UN Resolution
- **June 20** — World Refugee Day, recognized by the UN
- **June 21** — World Music Day, International Day of Yoga
- **June 23** — United Nations Public Service Day, recognized by the UN
- **June 26** — International Day in Support of Victims of Torture, recognized by the UN
- **3rd Sunday of June** — International Fathers' Day

July

- **July 1** — Doctors' Day, Bidhan Chandra Roy's Birth Day
- 1st Saturday of July — International Day of Cooperatives, recognized by the UN
- **July 1** — International Reggae Day - Jamaica
- **July 7** — International Cooperative Day
- **July 8** — Writer's Day
- **July 11** — World Population Day, recognized by the UN
- **July 23** — World Stress Down Day

August

- **August 12** — International Youth Day, recognized by the UN
- **August 13** — International Left handers Day
- **August 15** — Independence Day of India
- **August 19** — World Humanitarian Day

September

- **September 5** — Teacher's Day in India, Birth Day of Dr. Radhakrishnan
- **September 8** — International Literacy Day, recognized by the UN
- **September 10** — World Suicide Prevention Day
- **September 11** — 9/11 anniversary (World Trade Center Attack)
- **September 11** — World First Aid Day

- **September 15** — International Day of Democracy, recognized by the UN
- **September 19** — International Talk Like a Pirate Day
- **September 21** — International Day of Peace, recognized by the UN
- **September 21** — World Alzheimer's Day
- **September 22** — (World) Car Free Day
- **September 26** — European Day of Languages
- **September 27** — World Tourism Day

- **September 28** — Right to Know Day (RightToKnowDay.net)
- **September 28** — World Rabies Day
- **September 29** — International Hug A Gamer Day

October

- **First Monday** — World Habitat Day, recognized by the UN
- **October 1** — International Day of Older Persons, recognized by the UN
- **October 1** — World Vegetarian Day
- **October 2** — International Day of Non-Violence, recognized by the UN, observed on M.K. Gandhi's birthday
- **October 3** — World Smile Day
- **October 4** — World Animal's Day

- **October 5** — World Teachers' Day
- **October 9** — World Hospice and Palliative Care Day
- **October 8** — World Humanitarian Action Day
- **October 8** — World Egg Day - 2nd Friday of October every year
- **October 9** — World Post Day, recognized by the UN
- **October 9** — Global Jamie Day, recognized by the UN
- **October 10** — World Mental Health Day, recognized by the UN
- **October 10** — World Day Against Death Penalty, recognized by the WCADP

- **October 13** — International Suit Up Day
- **October 14** — World Standards Day
- **October 15** — World Blind Day / World Sight Day
- **October 15** — International Day of Rural Women, recognized by the UN
- **October 15** — Global Handwashing Day
- **October 16** — National Boss Day (Boss's Day)
- **October 16** — World Food Day, recognized by the UN

- **October 20** — International Day of the Air Traffic Controller
- **October 20** — World Statistics Day
- **October 24** — United Nations Day, recognized by the UN
- **October 24** — World Development Information Day, recognized by the UN

November

- **Third Sunday** — World Day of Remembrance for Road Traffic Victims, recognized by the UN
- **November 1** — World Vegan Day
- **November 8** — Paul's Day!
- **November 9** — World Freedom Day
- **November 10** — World Immunization Day
- **November 13** — World Kindness Day
- **November 14** — World Diabetes Day, recognized by the UN; Children's Day, Birthday of Pt. Jawaharlal Nehru, Prime Minister of India

- **November 16** — International Day for Tolerance, recognized by the UN
- **November 17** — International Students' Day
- **November 19** — World Toilet Day
- **November 20** — Universal Children's Day, recognized by the UN

- **November 21** — World Hello Day
- **November 21** — World Television Day, recognized by the UN
- **November 25** — International Day for the Elimination of Violence against Women, recognized by the UN
- **November 25** — International Meatless Day
- **November 29** — International Day of Solidarity with the Palestinian People, recognized by the UN
- **November 30** — Computer Security Day

December

- **December 1** — World AIDS Day, recognized by the UN

- **December 2** — International Day for the Abolition of Slavery
- **December 3** — International Day of Persons with Disabilities
- **December 5** — International Volunteer Day for Economic and Social Development
- **December 7** — International Civil Aviation Day
- **December 9** — The International Day against Corruption
- **December 10** — Human Rights Day
- **December 11** — International Mountain Day
- **December 17** — International Rabbit's Day
- **December 18** — International Migrants Day
- **December 19** — United Nations Day for South-South Cooperation

- **December 25** — Christmas

❑❑❑

International Organizations

3

An international organization, or more formally intergovernmental organization (IGO), is an organization that has sovereign states or other IGOs as members. Such organizations function according to the principles of intergovernmentalism, which means that unanimity is required. The European Union is, however, an exception to this rule in some areas.

Non-governmental organizations (NGOs) are private organizations that can also be international in scope. However, the term'international organization' is reserved for intergovernmental organizations only.

GLOBAL ORGANIZATIONS

- United Nations, its specialized agencies, and associated organizations
- Organization of the Islamic Conference, its specialized agencies, and associated organizations INTERPOL
- International Hydrographic Organization
- World Trade Organization
- International Red Cross and Red Crescent Movement

REGIONAL ORGANIZATIONS– EUROPE

- European Union (EU)
- Council of Europe (COE)
- Economic Commission for Europe (ECE)
- European Free Trade Association (EFT A)
- European Medicines Agency (EMEA)
- European Space Agency (ESA)
- European Patent Organization (EPO)

Asia

- Asia Cooperation Dialogue (ACD)
- Asian Development Bank (ADB)

- East Asian Summit (EAS)
- Association of Southeast Asian Nations (ASEAN)
- South Asian Association for Regional Cooperation (SAARC)
- Gulf Cooperation Council

Eurasia

- Commonwealth of Independent States (CIS)
- Shanghai Cooperation Organization (SCO)
- Eurasian Economic Community
- Central Asian Cooperation Organization

Africa

- African Union
- Economic Community of West African States (ECOWAS)
- Southern American Development Community (SADC)
- Arab Maghreb Union
- Organization of American States (OAS)
- South American Community of Nations
- Andean Community
- Caribbean Community (CARICOM)
- Central American Parliament
- Cooperation System of the American Air Forces (CSAAF)

Trans-atlantic

- North Atlantic Treaty Organization (NATO)
- Organization for Security and Cooperation in Europe (OSCE)

Arctic Ocean

- Arctic Council

Indian Ocean

- Indian Ocean Rim Association for Regional Cooperation (IOR-ARC)
- Indian Ocean Commission (IOC)

Pacific

- Asia-Pacific Economic Cooperation (APEC)
- Pacific Islands Forum
- Secretariat of the Pacific Community (SPC)

IMPORTANT ORGANIZATIONS

United Nations

The United Nations is an international organization founded in 1945 after the Second World War by 51 countries committed to maintaining international peace and security, developing friendly relations among nations and promoting social progress, better living standards and human rights.

Due to its unique international character, and the powers vested in its founding Charter, the Organization can take action on a wide range of issues, and provide a forum for its 193 Member States to express their views.

The work of the United Nations reaches every corner of the globe. Although best known for peacekeeping, peace-building, conflict prevention and humanitarian assistance, there are many other ways the United Nations and its System (specialized agencies, funds and programmes) affect our lives and make the world a better place.

The organization works on a broad range of fundamental issues, from sustainable development, environment and refugees protection, disaster relief, counter terrorism, disarmament and non-proliferation, to promoting democracy, human rights, gender equality and the advancement of women, governance, economic and social development and international health, clearing land-mines, expanding food production, and more, in order to achieve its goals and coordinate efforts for a safer world for this and future generations.

Aims

- To keep peace throughout the world
- To develop friendly relations among nations
- To help nations work together to improve the lives of poor people, to conquer hunger, disease and illiteracy and to encourage respect for each others' rights and freedoms

STRUCTURE OF GENERAL ASSEMBLY

The General Assembly is the main deliberative assembly of the United Nations. Composed of all United Nations member states, the assembly meets in regular yearly sessions under a President elected from among the member states. Over a two-week period at the start of each session, all members have the opportunity to address the assembly. Traditionally, the Secretary-General makes the first statement, followed by the President of the assembly. The first session was convened on 10 January 1946 in the Westminster Central Hall in London and included representatives of 51 nations.

SECURITY COUNCIL

It is charged with responsibility of maintaining peace and security among nations. While other organs of the United Nations only make recommendations to member governments, the Security Council has the power to make decisions that member governments must carry out under the United Nations Charter. The decisions of the Council are known as United Nations Security Council Resolutions. The Security Council is made up 15 member states, consisting of five permanent seats and ten temporary seats. The permanent five are China, France, Russia, the United Kingdom and the United States.

SECRETARIAT

The United Nations Secretariat is headed by the Secretary-General, assisted by a staff of international civil servants worldwide. It provides studies, information, and facilities needed by United Nations bodies for their meetings. It also carries out tasks as directed by the UN Security Council, the UN General Assembly, the UN Economic and Social Council, and other UN bodies.

INTERNATIONAL COURT OF JUSTICE (ICJ)

The International Court of Justice (ICJ), located in The Hague, Netherlands, is the primary judicial organ of the United Nations. Established in 1945 by the United Nations Charter, the Court began work in 1946 as the successor to the Permanent Court of International Justice. The Statute of the International Court of Justice, similar to that of its predecessor, is the main constitutional document constituting and regulating the Court.

It is based in the Peace Palace in The Hague, Netherlands. Its purpose is to adjudicate disputes among states. The court has heard cases related to war crimes, illegal state interference and ethnic cleansing, among others, and continues to hear cases.

ECONOMIC AND SOCIAL COUNCIL

The Economic and Social Council (ECOSOC) assists the General Assembly in promoting international economic and social cooperation and development. ECOSOC has 54 members, all of which are elected by the General Assembly for a three-year term. The President is elected for a one-year term and chosen amongst the small or middle powers represented on ECOSOC. ECOSOC is well-positioned to provide policy coherence and coordinate the overlapping functions of the UN's subsidiary bodies and it is in these roles that it is most active.

SPECIALIZED INSTITUTIONS

Specialized agencies are autonomous organizations of the United Nations that work with the UN and each other through the Economic and Social Council. Specialized agencies may or may not have been originally created by the United Nations, but they are incorporated into the United Nations System by the United Nations Economic and Social Council acting under Articles 57 and 63 of the United Nations Charter. At present the UN has in total 15 specialized agencies that carry out various functions on behalf of the UN. These agencies function to work on particular issues. Some of the most well-known agencies are the International Atomic Energy Agency, the Food and Agriculture Organization, UNESCO (United Nations Educational, Scientific and Cultural Organization), the World Bank and the World Health Organization.

It is through these agencies that the UN performs most of its humanitarian work. Examples include mass vaccination programmes (through the WHO), the avoidance of famine and malnutrition (through the work of the WFP) and the protection of vulnerable and displaced people (for example, by the UNHCR). The United Nations Charter stipulates that each primary organ of the UN can establish various specialized agencies to fulfil its duties.

LANGUAGES

The UN has six official languages: Arabic, Chinese, English, French, Russian and Spanish.

INTERPOL

International Criminal Police Organization – INTERPOL is an organization facilitating international police cooperation. It was established as the International Criminal Police Commission in 1923 and adopted its telegraphic address as its common name in 1956. The organization's headquarters is in Lyon, France. It is the second largest intergovernmental organization after the United Nations.

Its membership of 188 countries provides finance of around $59 million through annual contributions. Interpol's constitution forbids its involvement in any political, military, religious, or racial crimes. Its work focuses primarily on public safety, terrorism, organized crime, crimes against humanity, environmental crime, genocide, war crimes, piracy, illicit drug production, drug trafficking, weapons smuggling, human trafficking, money laundering, child pornography, white-collar crime, computer crime, intellectual property crime and corruption.

INTERNATIONAL HYDROGRAPHIC ORGANIZATION

The International Hydrographic Organization (IHO) is the inter-governmental Organization representing the hydrographic community. It enjoys observer status at the UN and is its recognised competent authority on hydrographic surveying and nautical charting. When referring to hydrography and nautical charting in Conventions and similar Instruments, it is the IHO standards and specifications that are normally used.

INTERNATIONAL RED CROSS AND RED CRESCENT MOVEMENT

The International Red Cross and Red Crescent Movement is an international humanitarian movement with approximately 97 million volunteers, members and staff worldwide which was founded to protect human life and health, to ensure respect for all human beings, and to preventandalleviatehumansuffering, withoutanydiscriminationbased on nationality, race, sex, religious beliefs, class or political opinions.

The movement consists of several distinct organizations that are legally independent from each other, but are united within the movement through common basic principles, objectives, symbols, statutes and governing organs.

WORLD TRADE ORGANIZATION

The World Trade Organization (WTO) is an international organization designed to supervise and liberalize international trade. It came into being on

January 1, 1995, and is the successor to the General Agreement on Tariffs and Trade (GATT), which was created in 1947. It deals with the rules of trade between nations at a global or near-global level. It is responsible for negotiating and implementing new trade agreements, and is in charge of policing member countries' adherence to all the WTO's agreements, signed by the bulk of the world's trading nations and ratified in their parliaments. Most of the WTO's current work comes from the 1986-94 negotiations called the Uruguay Round.

The organization is governed by a Ministerial Conference,which meets every two years; a General Council, which implements the conference's policy decisions and is responsible for day-to-day administration; and a director-general, who is appointed by the Ministerial Conference. The WTO's headquarters are in Geneva, Switzerland.

UNIVERSAL POSTAL UNION

Established in 1874, the Universal Postal Union (UPU), with its headquarters in the Swiss capital Berne, is the second oldest international organization worldwide. With its 191 member countries, the UPU is the primary forum for cooperation between postal sector players. It helps to ensure a truly universal network of up-to-date products and services. It fulfils an advisory, mediating and liaison role, and provides technical assistance where needed. It sets the rules for international mail exchanges and makes recommendations to stimulate growth in mail, parcel and financial services volumes and improve quality of service for customers.

The UPU consists of four bodies:

- The Congress
- The Council of Administration (CA)
- The Postal Operations Council (POC)
- The International Bureau (IB)

Two cooperatives:

- Telematics Cooperative
- EMS Cooperative

The UPU established that:

1. There should be a uniform flat rate to mail a letter anywhere in the world.
2. Postal authorities should give equal treatment to foreign and domestic mail.

3. Each country should retain all money it has collected for international postage.

EUROPEAN UNION

The European Union (EU) is an economic and political union of 27 member states which are located primarily in Europe. The EU traces its origins from the European Coal and Steel Community (ECSC) and the European Economic Community (EEC) formed by six countries in the 1950s. In the intervening years the EU has grown in size by the accession of new member states, and in power by the addition of policy areas to its remit. The Maastricht Treaty established the European Union under its current name in 1993. The last amendment to the constitutional basis of the EU, the Treaty of Lisbon, came into force in 2009.

Operations

The EU operates through a hybrid system of supranational independent institutions and inter-governmentally made decisions negotiated by the member states. The important institutions of the EU include:

- The European Commission,
- The Council of the European Union,
- The European Council,
- The Court of Justice of the European Union, and
- The European Central Bank.

The European Parliament is elected every five years by EU citizens. The EU has developed a single market through a standardised system of laws which apply in all member states including the abolition of passport

controls within the Schengen area. It ensures the free movement of people, goods, services, and capital, enacts legislation in justice and home affairs, and maintains common policies on trade, agriculture, fisheries and regional development. A monetary union, the eurozone, wasestablishedin 1999 and is currently composed of seventeen member states. Through the Common Foreign and Security Policy the EU has developed a limited role in external relations and defence. Permanent diplomatic missions have been established around the world and the EU is represented at the United Nations, the WTO, the G8 and the G-20.

With a combined population of 500 million inhabitants, the EU generated an estimated 21% (US$ 14.8 trillion) share of the global economy (GDP PPP) in 2009. As a trading bloc the EU accounts for 20% of global imports and exports.

On 1 January 2007, Romania and Bulgaria became the EU's newest members. In the same year Slovenia adopted the euro, followed in 2008 by Cyprus and Malta, by Slovakia in 2009 and by Estonia in 2011. In June 2009, the 2009 Parliament elections were held leading to a renewal of Barroso's Commission Presidency, and in July 2009 Iceland formally applied for EU membership.

On 1 December 2009, the Lisbon Treaty come into force and reformed many aspects of the EU. In particular it changed the legal structure of the European Union, merging the EU three pillars system into asingle legalentity provisioned with legalpersonality, andit created a permanent President of the European Council, the first of which is Herman Van Rompuy, and a strengthened High Representative,

ASEAN

The Association of Southeast Asian Nations, commonly abbreviated ASEAN, is a geo-political and economic organization of 10 countries located in Southeast Asia, which was formed on 8 August 1967 by Indonesia, Malaysia, the Philippines, Singapore and Thailand. Since then, membership has expanded to include Brunei, Burma (Myanmar), Cambodia, Laos, and Vietnam. Its aims include the acceleration of economic growth, social progress, cultural development among its members, the protection of the peace and stability of the region, and to provide opportunities for member countries to discuss differences peacefully.

ASEAN spans over an area of 4.46 million km, 2, 3% of the total land area of the Earth, with a population of approximately 600 million people, 8.8% of the world population. In 2010, its combined nominal GDP had grown to USD $1.8 trillion. If ASEAN were a single country, it would rank as the 9th largest economy in the world and the 3rd largest in Asia in terms of nominal GDP.

On 15 December 1995, the Southeast Asian Nuclear-Weapon-Free Zone Treaty was signed with the intention of turning Southeast Asia into a Nuclear-Weapon-Free Zone. The treaty took effect on 28 March 1997 after all but one of the member states have ratified it. It became fully effective on 21 June 2001, after the Philippines ratified it, effectively banning all nuclear weapons in the region.

Early 2011, Timor Leste plans to submit a letter of application to the

ASEAN Secretariat in Indonesia to be the eleventh member of ASEAN at the summit in Jakarta. Indonesia has shown a warm welcome to Timor Leste.

The Organization hosts cultural activities in an attempt to further integrate the region. These include sports and educational activities as well as writing awards.

SOUTH ASIAN ASSOCIATION FOR REGIONAL COOPERATION (SAARC)

The South Asian Association for Regional Cooperation (SAARC) is an organization of South Asian nations, founded in December 1985 and dedicated to economic, technological, social, and cultural development emphasizing collective self-reliance. Its seven founding members are Bangladesh, Bhutan, India, the Maldives, Nepal, Pakistan, and Sri Lanka. Afghanistan joined the organization in 2007. Meetings of heads of state are usually scheduled annually; meetings of foreign secretaries, twice annually. It is headquartered in Kathmandu, Nepal.

Objectives

The objectives of the Association as defined in the Charter are:

- to promote the welfare of the people of South Asia and to improve their quality of life;
- to accelerate economic growth, social progress and cultural development in the region and to provide all individuals the opportunity to live in dignity and to realize their full potential;
- to promote and strengthen collective self-reliance among the countries of South Asia;
- to contribute to mutual trust, understanding and appreciation of one another's problems;
- to promote active collaboration and mutual assistance in the economic, social, cultural, technical and scientific fields;
- to strengthen cooperation with other developing countries;
- to strengthen cooperation among themselves in international forums on matters of common interest; and
- to cooperate with international and regional organizations with similar aims and purposes.

The SAARC Secretariat and Member States observe 8 December as the SAARC Charter Day.

SAARC has intentionally laid more stress on"core issues" mentioned above rather than more decisive political issues like the Kashmir dispute and the Sri Lankan civil war.

SOUTH ASIAN FREE TRADE AREA (SAFTA)

The Agreement on the South Asian Free Trade Area is an agreement reached at the 12th SAARC summit at Islamabad, capital of Pakistan on 6 January 2004. It creates a framework for the creation of a free trade area covering 1.6 billion people in India, Pakistan, Nepal, Sri Lanka, Bangladesh, Bhutan and the Maldives. The seven foreign ministers of the region signed a framework agreement on SAFTA with zero customs duty on the trade of practically all products in the region by end 2016. The new agreement, i.e., SAFTA, came into being on 1 January 2006 and will be operational following the ratification of the agreement by the seven governments. SAFTA requires the developing countries in South Asia, that is, India, Pakistan and Sri Lanka, to bring their duties down to 20 per cent in the first phase of the two year period ending in 2007. In the final five year phase ending 2012, the 20 per cent duty is said be reduced to zero in a series of annual cuts. The least developed nations in South Asia consisting of Nepal, Bhutan, Bangladesh and Maldives had an additional three years to reduce tariffs to zero. India and Pakistan have signed but not ratified the treaty.

FREE TRADE AGREEMENT

Over the years, the SAARC members have expressed their unwillingness on signing a free trade agreement. Though India has several trade pacts with Maldives, Nepal, Bhutan and Sri Lanka, similar trade agreements with Pakistan and Bangladesh have been stalled due to political and economic concerns on both sides. India has been constructing a barrier across its borders with Bangladesh and Pakistan. In 1993, SAARC countries signed an agreement to gradually lower tariffs withintheregion, in Dhaka. Eleven years later, at the 12th SAARC Summit at Islamabad, SAARC countries devised the South Asia Free Trade Agreement which created a framework for the establishment of a free trade area covering 1.6 billion people. This agreement went into force on January 1, 2008. Under this agreement, SAARC members will bring their duties down to 20 per cent by 2009. Last summit was held in Thimphu on 28-29 April, 2010 and next is planned in November 2011.

ECONOMIC COOPERATION ORGANIZATION

The Economic Cooperation Organization (ECO) is an intergovernmental organization involving seven Asian and three Eurasian nations. It provides a platform to discuss ways to improve development and promote trade, and investment opportunities. The ECO is an ad hoc organization under the United Nations Charter (Chap. VIII). The common objective is to establish a single market for goods and services, much like the European Union. ECO's secretariat and cultural department are located in Tehran, its economic bureau is in Turkey and its scientific bureau is situated in Pakistan. The organization's population is 416,046,863 and the area is 8,620,697 km^2. The organization was founded by Turkey, Iran and Pakistan.

SECRETARIAT OF THE PACIFIC COMMUNITY

The Secretariat of the Pacific Community, or SPC (sometimes Pacific Community), is a regional intergovernmental organization whose membershipincludesbothnations andterritories. It aimsto"develop the technical, professional, scientific, research, planning and management capability of Pacific Island people and directly provide information and advice, to enable them to make informed decisions about their future development and well-being."

❑❑❑

Timeline of Indian and World History

4

STONE AGE

Rock Shelters of Bhimbetka (9000-7000 BC)

The Rock Shelters of Bhimbetka in the foothills of the Vindhyan Mountains on the southern edge of the central Indian plateau. Within massive sandstone outcrops, above comparatively dense forest, are five clusters of natural rock shelters, displaying paintings that appear to date from the Mesolithic Period right through to the historical period. The site is a U.N. World Heritage site.

Mehrgarh Culture (7000-3300 BC)

- **7000 BC:** Mehrgarh Culture (Period I) begins, which was one of the world's earliest Neolithic cultures
- **5500 BC:** Period II of Mehrgarh begins
- **4800 BC:** Period III of Mehrgarh begins
- **3500 BC:** Period IV of Mehrgarh begins
- **3300 BC:** Period IV of Mehrgarh ends.

BRONZE AGE

Indus Valley Civilization (2800-1900 BC)

- **3300 BC:** Antecedents of the Indus Valley Civilization begin with the Ravi phase, eventually becoming one of the world's three earliest urban civilizations, contemporary to Mesopotamia and Ancient Egypt.
- **2800 BC:** Kot Diji phase of the Indus Valley Civilization begins. The civilization used an early form of the Indus signs, the so-called Indus script.

- **2600 BC:** Mature Harappan phase of the Indus Valley Civilization begins. The cities of Harappa, Lothal, Kalibangan, Dholavira, Rakhigarhi and Mohenjo-daro become large metropolises and the civilization expands to over 2,500 cities and settlements across what is now Pakistan, much of northwestern and western India, and parts of Afghanistan and Iran.
- **1700 BC:** Indus Valley Civilization comes to an end but is continued by the Cemetery H culture and other cultures.

Vedic Era (1500-500 BC)

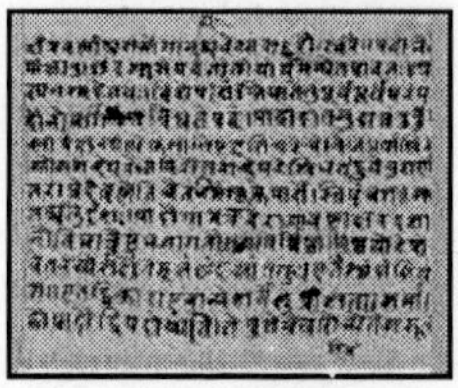

- **1500-1000 BCE:** Rigveda
- **1500-1000 BCE:** Early Vedic period
- **1000-500 BCE:** Later Vedic period
- **1300 BC:** Cemetery H culture comes to an end

IRON AGE

- **1000 BC:** Iron Age of India

- **600 BC:** Sixteen Maha Janapadas ("Great Realms" or "Great Kingdoms") emerge. A number of these Mahajana-padasaresemi-democratic "republics", rather than oligarchies.
- **500 BC:** Vedic Civilization comes to an end after the Historical Vedic religion evolves into early classical Hinduism.
- **599 BC:** Mahavira, 24th Tirthankar of Jainism was born.
- **563 BC:**Siddhartha Gautama, founder of Buddhism was born as a prince of the Shakya tribe, which ruled parts of what is now Northern Bihar and Southern Nepal in Ancient India.
- **538 BC:**Cyrus the Great, founder of the Persian Achaemenid Empire, conquers northwestern parts of the Indian subcontinent.
- **350 BC:** Panini, a resident of Gandhara, describes the grammar and morphology of Sanskrit in the text Ashtadhyayi. Panini's standardized Sanskrit is known as Classical Sanskrit.

- **333 BC:** Persian rule in the northwest ends after Darius III is defeated by Alexander the Great, who establishes the Macedonian Empire after inheriting the Persian Achaemenid Empire.
- **326 BC:** Ambhi king of Taxila surrenders to Alexander.
- **321 BC:** Mauryan Empire was founded by Chandragupta Maurya in Magadha after he defeated the Nanda dynasty and Macedonian Seleucid Empire. The capital city was Patliputra (Modern Patna in Bihar)
- **305 BC:** Chandragupta Maurya defeats Seleucus Nicator of the Seleucid Empire.
- **304 BC:** Seleucus gives up his territories in the subcontinent (Afghanistan/Baluchistan) to Chandragupta in ex- change for 500 elephants. Seleucus offers his daughter in marriage to Chandragupta to seal their friendship.
- **273 BC:** Ashoka the Great, regarded as the greatest ancient Indian emperor, grandson of Chandragupta Maurya, ascends as emperor of the Mauryan Empire.

- **266 BC:** Ashoka conquers and unifies most of South Asia, along with Afghanistan and eastern Iran.
- **265 BC:** Kalinga War took place between Ashoka and the kingdom of Kalinga.
- **232 BC:** Ashoka dies and is succeeded by Kunala.
- **230 BC:** Simuka declares independence from Mauryan rule and establishes the Satavahana Empire.
- **200 BC:** Kuninda Kingdom established.
- **200-100 BC:** Tholkappiyam describes the grammar and morphology of Tamil; it is the oldest existing Tamil grammar (dates vary between 200 BCE and 100 CE).
- **184 BC:** The Mauryan Empire, which shrunk considerably, collapsedafteritsemperor Brihadrathawasassassinated by his Brahmin general Pusyamitra Sunga, who then established the Sunga dynasty.

- **180 BC:** Establishment of the Indo-Greek kingdom.
- **80 BC:** Establishment of the Indo-Scythian kingdom.
- **57 BC:** Beginning of Vikram Era.
- **10 BC:** Establishment of the Indo-Parthian kingdom.
- **78 AD:** Gautamiputra Satkarni becomes Satavahana emperor and starts Shatvahana era calendar after defeating Scythian king Vikramaditya.
- **35 AD:** Western Satraps formed.
- **240 AD:** Sri-Gupta starts the Gupta Empire in Magadha, with its capital in Patliputra.
- **320 AD:** Chandragupta I ascends to the Gupta throne.
- **335 AD:** Samudragupta ascends the Gupta throne and expands the empire.
- **380 AD:** Chandragupta II, Samudragupta's son, becomes the Gupta emperor.
- **450 AD:** Invasions by the Hunas.

Medieval India (550-1526 AD)

- **606 AD:** Harshavardhana crowned as king. Bhaskarbharman of Kamrupa kingdom was his contemporary.
- **637 AD:** Badami Chalukya power at its peak. Pulakesin II pushes north up to the Narmada and defeats the invading Harshavardhana of Kannauj.
- **712 AD:** First Muslim, Md. Bin Qasim, defeats King Dahir.
- **788 AD:** Adi Shankara born in Kalady, in central Kerala.
- **814 AD:** Nripatunga Amoghavarsha I becomes Rashtrakuta king.
- **836 - 910:** Gurjara-Pratihara Dynasty ruled.
- **1000:** Invasion of Mahmud of Ghazni.
- **1021:** Mahmud Ghazni defeats Tarnochalpal and annexes Punjab.
- **1030:** Alberuni arrives in India; Death of Mahmud of Ghazni.
- **1058:** Sumra Dynasty ends the Arab domination and establishes its own rule over Sindh.

- **1120:** Kalyani Chalukya power at its peak. Vikramaditya VI ushers in Vikrama Chalukya era.
- **1157:** The Kalachuris under Bijjala II capture Kalyani.
- **1191:** Victory of Prithviraj Chauhan. First battle of Tarain between Mohammed Ghori and Prithviraj III; Ghauri is defeated by Prithivi Raj Chauhan III.
- **1192:** Victory of Mohammed Ghori. Second battle of Tarain fought between Ghori and Prithivi Raj Chauhan.
- **1194:** Battle of Chandawar fought between Ghori and Jayachandra; Ghori defeated Jayachandra and killed him.
- **1206:** Gakkhars kill Muhammad Ghori during a raid on his camp on the Jhelum River.
- **1221:** Genghis Khan invades Punjab.
- **1310:** Ala-ud-din Khilji's army under Malik Kafur occupies Devagiri, ending the Seuna Yadava Kingdom.
- **1323:** Ulugh Khan defeats Pratapa Rudra ending the Kakatiya dynasty.
- **1336:** Vijayanagara Empire established by Harihara I and his brother Bukka Raya I.
- **1343:** Veera Ballala III killed at the Battle of Madurai.
- **1347:** Governor Hasan Gangu revolts against Muhammad bin Tughluq, founding the Bahmani Sultanate.
- **1351:** Samma Dynasty assumes rule over Sindh.
- **1370:** Bukka, the Vijayanagara ruler, and his son Kumara Kamapna capture the entire Tamil-speaking parts.
- **1398:** Timur plunders Lahore.
- **1401:** Dilawar Khan establishes the Malwa Sultanate in present-day northern India.
- **1407:** Zafar Khan, governor of Gujarat, declares himself as Sultan Muzaffar Shah, founding the Gujarat Sultanate/ Muzaffarid dynasty.
- **1414:** Khizr Khan, deputized by Timur to be the governor of Multan, takes over Delhi founding the Sayyid dynasty
- **1424:** Deva Raya II succeeded his father Veera Vijaya Bukka Raya as monarch of the Vijayanagara Empire

- **1443:** Abdur Razzaq visits India
- **1446:** Mallikarjuna Raya succeeds his father Deva Raya II
- **1451:** Bahlul Khan Lodhi ascends the throne of Delhi sultanate, starting the Lodhi dynasty
- **1469:** Guru Nanak, the founder of Sikhism, was born
- **1483:** Birth of Babur in Andijan, Fergana Valley in Central Asia

Guru Nanak Dev

- **1485:** Saluva Narasimha Deva Raya drives out Praudha Raya, ending the Sangama Dynasty
- **1486:** Sher Shah Suri (original name Farid Khan) born in Sasaram Guru Nanak Dev
- **1490:** Ahmadnagar declares independence, followed by Bijapur and Berar in the same year, thus breaking up the Bahmani Sultanate.
- **1497–1499:** Vasco de Gama's first voyage from Europe to India and back
- **1503:** Kingdom of Kochi is taken over by the Portuguese, creating the first European settlement in India..
- **1508:** The Christian-Islamic power struggle, in Europe and the Middle East, spills over into the Indian Ocean as Battle of Chaul, during the Portuguese-Mamluk War

- **1509:** Battle of Diu marks the beginning of the dominance of the Europeans in the Asian naval theater.
- **1522:** Portuguese land on the Coromandel Coast.

Post-Medieval Era (1526-1857)

- **1526:** Sultan Ibrahim Lodi, of the Delhi Sultanate, angers local nobles, who respond by inviting Babur, the Mughal ruler of Kabul, to invade Delhi and Agra. The local population, plus the possession of artillery, assists Babur in killing the Sultan (whose soldiers desert him) at the Battle of Panipat.

- **1527:** Babur bribes Mewar general Silhadi promising him a kingdom, and Silhadi betrays Mewar King Rana Sanga in the Battle of Khanwa, thus leading to the annexation of Mewar.

- **1530:** Babur completes his Baburnama, reflecting on society, politics, economics, history, geography, nature, flora and fauna, which to this day is a standard textbook in 25 countries. Babur dies, and is succeeded by his son Humayun.
- **1539:** Battle of Chausa fought between Humayun and Sher Shah Suri in which Humayun was defeated and fled.
- **1540:** Battle of Kannauj fought between Humayun and Sher Shah Suri, and Humayun was completely defeated. Humayun lost the Mughal empire to Afghans (Suri Dynasty), and passed 12 years in exile.
- **1545:** Death of Sher Shah Suri, succeeded by Islam Shah.
- **1554:** Death of Islam Shah.
- **1555:** Humayun regained the throne of Delhi from the hands of weak successors of Sher Shah.
- **1556:** Humayun converts from Sunni Islam to Shia Islam, to gain the alliance of the Shah of Persia. Humayun dies, and is succeeded by his son Akbar.

- **1556:** Hindu warrior Hemu, winner of 22 battles, defeats Akbar's forces at Agra and Delhi and establishes 'Hindu Raj' in North India, and bestowed with title of "Samrat Hem Chandra Vikramaditya"; Second Battle of Panipat fought between Hemu, the Hindu Vikramaditya, and Akbar's forces in which Hemu gets killed.
- **1565:** Battle of Talikota results in the rout of Vijayanagara empire.
- **1572:** Akbar annexes Gujarat, also shifts the Mughal capital to Fatehpur Sikri where a new township and citadel containing buildings of a unique all-India character— inspired by the architecture of Bengal, Gujarat, Malwa, Kashmir as well as the Timurid world—is born.

- **1574:** Akbar annexes Bengal.
- **1586:** Akbar annexes Kashmir.
- **1600:** East India company is formed in England. Gets exclusive trading rights with India.
- **1605:** Akbar dies, and is succeeded by his son Jehangir.
- **1628:** Jehangir announces"Chain of Justice"outside his palace that anyone can ring the bell and get a personal hearing with the emperor. Jehangir dies, and is succeeded by his son Shah Jahan.
- **1630:** Birth of Shivaji.
- **1644:** Shivaji takes oath of Independence at Raireshwar.
- **1658:** Shah Jahan completes Taj Mahal, Jama Masjid, and Red Fort. Imperial treasuries drained by architectural and military over-expenditures. Shah Jahan dies, and is succeeded by his son Aurangzeb.

- **1659:** Shivaji's ill-equipped and small Maratha army defeats mighty Adilshahi troops at the Battle of Pratapgarh in a major upset in Indian history. Shivaji personally kills Adilshahi commander Afzal Khan.
- **1674:** Forces led by Shivaji defeat Aurangzeb's troops, and establishes Maratha Empire.
- **1675:** Guru Tegh Bahadur, the ninth Guru of Sikhs is executed in Delhi by the order of Aurangzeb for his support for the Kashmiri Hindus to practice their religion.

- **1680:** Shivaji dies of fever at Raigad.
- **1681:** Aurangzeb invades the Deccan
- **1699:** Guru Gobind Singh, the 10th Guru of Sikhs, creates Khalsa, the saint-soldier at Anandpur Sahib, Punjab.
- **1749:** The Maratha Peshwa (prime minister) usurps the Maratha kingdom, starting a new dynastic rule based in Pune.

- **1757:** Battle of Plassey
- **1760:** Marathas comprehensively defeat the Nizam, Maratha Empire reaches its zenith.
- **1761:** The Marathas are routed in the Third Battle of Panipat on 14 January 1761, by the Afghans led by Ahmad Shah Durrani, an ethnic Pashtun, also known as Ahmad Shah Abdali. The battle is considered one of the largest battles fought in the 18th century.
- **1764:** Battle of Buxar
- **1773:** Narayanrao Peshwa is murdered by his uncle Raghunathrao's wife in front of Raghunathrao.
- **1774:** Chief Justice of the Maratha Empire, Ram Shastri, passes death sentence against the ruling Peshwa Raghunathrao for murdering his nephew.
- **1777:** First Anglo-Maratha War begins, in which Haidar Ali of Mysore defeats the combined armies of the East India Company, the Marathas and the Nizam of Hyderabad.
- **1779:** Maratha sardar Mahadji Shinde routs the East India Company army in the Battle of Wadgaon. War ends with the restoration of status quo as per Treaty of Salbai.
- **1780:** Second Anglo-Mysore War begins.
- **1784:** War ends with the Treaty of Mangalore.
- **1789:** Third Anglo-Mysore War begins.
- **1790:** The Marathas under Holkar and General de Boigne defeat the Rajputs of Jaipur and Mughals at the Battle of Patan, where 3000+ Rajput cavalry is killed and the entire Mughal unit vanquished. The defeat crushes Rajput hope of independence from external influence

- **1792:** Third Anglo-Mysore War ends.
- **1796:** Ching-Thang Khomba moves Manipur's capital to Kangla
- **1798:** Fourth Anglo-Mysore War begins.

- **1799:** Fourth Anglo-Mysore War ends with the death of Tipu Sultan, the victory of the East India Company, and the restoration of their ally, the Wodeyar dynasty of Mysore.
- **1799:** Polygar War
- **1801:** Maharaja Ranjit Singh establishes Khalsa rule of Punjab from Lahore. Khalsa army liberates Kashmiri Pundits and invades Afghanistan through Khyber Pass.
- **1803:** Second Anglo-Maratha War begins
- **1805:** Second Anglo-Maratha War ends
- **1806:** Vellore Mutiny
- **1807:** East India Company signs treaty of Amritsar with Maharaja Ranjit Singh
- **1817:** Third Anglo-Maratha War begins
- **1818:** Third Anglo-Maratha War ends with the defeat of Bajirao II and the end of the Maratha Empire leaving the East India Company with control of almost the whole of India
- **1823-26:** Anglo–Burmese Wars
- **1839:** Anglo-Afghan War
- **1845-49:** Anglo-Sikh Wars
- **1857:** Indian Rebellion of 1857
- **1858–1947:** British Raj
- **1947:** India got independence and Partition of India

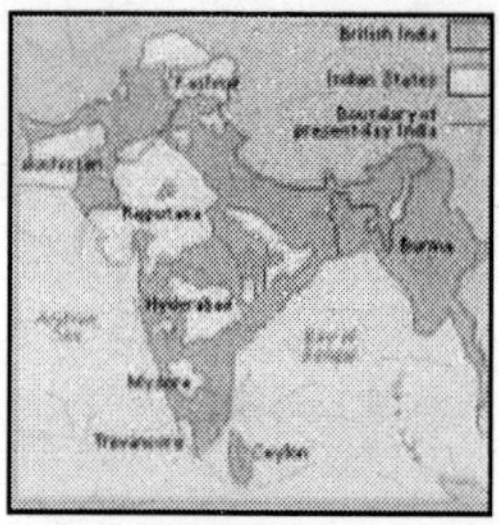

Post-Partition (1947 - Present)

- **1948:** Mahatma Gandhi assassinated by a nationalist.
- **1948:** War with Pakistan over disputed territory of Kashmir.
- **1948:** Telangana and other princely states integrated in Indian union
- **1951-52:** Congress Party wins first general elections under leadership of Jawaharlal Nehru

REGIONAL TENSIONS

- **1962:** India loses the brief border war with China.
- **1964:** Death of Prime Minister Jawaharlal Nehru.
- **1964:** Lal Bahadur Shastri became Indian Prime Minister.
- **1965:** Second war with Pakistan over Kashmir.
- **1966:** Nehru's daughter Indira Gandhi becomes prime minister.
- **1971:** Third war with Pakistan over creation of Bangladesh, formerly East Pakistan.
- **1974:** India explodes first nuclear device in underground test. Democratic strains
- **1975:** Indira Gandhi declares state of emergency after being found guilty of electoral malpractice.
- **1975-77:** Nearly 1,000 political opponents imprisoned and programme of compulsory birth control introduced.
- **1977:** Indira Gandhi's Congress Party loses general elections.
- **1980:** Indira Gandhi returns to power heading Congress party splinter group, Congress (Indira).

- **1984:** Troops storm Golden Temple - Sikhs' most holy shrine - to flush out Sikh militants pressing for self-rule.
- **1984:** Indira Gandhi assassinated by Sikh bodyguards, following which her son, Rajiv, takes over.
- **1987:** India deploys troops for peacekeeping operation in Sri Lanka's ethnic conflict.
- **1989:** Falling public support leads to Congress defeat in general election.
- **1990:** Muslim separatist groups begin campaign of violence in Kashmir.
- **1991:** Rajiv Gandhi assassinated by suicide bomber sympathetic to Sri Lanka's Tamil Tigers.
- **1992:** Hindu extremists demolish mosque in Ayodhya, triggering widespread Hindu-Muslim violence.

- **1996:** Congress suffers worst ever electoral defeat as Hindu nationalist BJP emerges as largest single party.
- **1998:** BJP forms coalition government under Prime Minister Atal Behari Vajpayee.
- **1998:** India carries out nuclear tests, leading to widespread international condemnation.
- **1999:** (February) Vajpayee makes historic bus trip to Pakistan to meet Premier Nawaz Sharif and to sign bilateral Lahore peace declaration.
- **1999:** (October) Cyclone devastates eastern state of Orissa, leaving at least 10,000 dead.
- **2000:** (May) India marks the birth of its billionth citizen.
- **2000:** US President Bill Clinton makes a groundbreaking visit to improve ties.
- **2001:** (January) Massive earthquakes hit the western state of Gujarat, leaving at least 30,000 dead.

- **2001:** (July) Vajpayee meets Pakistani President Pervez Musharraf in Agra to solve the Kashmir problem, known as Agra Summit. The meeting failed.
- **2001:** (July) Vajpayee's BJP party declines his offer to resign over a number of political scandals and the apparent failure of his talks with Pakistani President Musharraf.
- **2001:** (October) India fires on Pakistani military posts in the heaviest firing along the dividing line of control in Kashmir for almost a year.
- **2001:** (December) India, Pakistan mass troops on common border amid mounting fears of a looming war.
- **2002:** (January) India successfully test-fires a nuclear-capable ballistic missile - the Agni - off its eastern coast.

- **2002:** (July) Retired scientist and architect of India's missile programme APJ Abdul Kalam is elected president.
- **2003:** (August) At least 50 people are killed in two simultaneous bomb blasts in Bombay.
- **2004:** Manmohan Singh becomes Prime Minister
- **2006:** (March) US and India sign a nuclear agreement during a visit by US President George W Bush. The US gives India access to civilian nuclear technology while India agrees to greater scrutiny for its nuclear programme.

- **2007:** (February) India and Pakistan sign an agreement aimed at reducing the risk of accidental nuclear war.
- **2007:** (April) India's first commercial space rocket is launched, carrying an Italian satellite.
- **2007:** (July) Pratibha Patil becomes first woman to be elected president of India.

- **2008:** October - Following approval by the US Congress, President George W Bush sign to law a nuclear deal with India, which ends a three-decade ban on US nuclear trade with Delhi. India successfully launches its first mission to the moon, the unmanned lunar probe Chandrayaan-1.

- **2009:** (February) India and Russia sign deals worth $700m, according to which Moscow will supply uranium to Delhi.
- **2010:** (October) XIX Commonwealth Games were held in Delhi, India, from 3 to 14 October 2010.

- **2011:** (January) The Indian musical (music director) who has been nominated for Oscar

Awards this year is A. R. Rahman. He has been nominated for his music in Dannny Boy's film '127 Hours' in the categories of Best Song and Best Original Score trophy for Oscar Awards this year.

- **2011:** April 02, The 2011, ICC Cricket World Cup was the tenth Cricket World Cup. The series was won by India after 28 years who defeated Sri Lanka by 6 wickets in the final. India became the first nation to win a World Cup final on home soil. Indian captain Mahendra Singh Dhoni scored an unbeaten 91 in the final and was adjudged the man of the match. India's Yuvraj Singh was declared the man of the series.

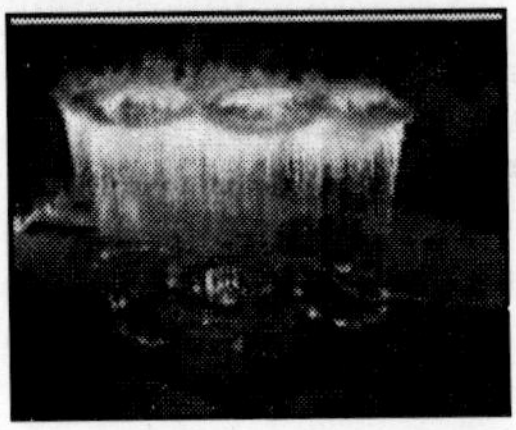

- **2012:** On July 27, London officially kicked-off the world's biggest sporting event with a star-studded opening ceremony that felt part Broadway musical and part history lesson. When it was all over, the United States took a familiar spot atop the overall medal tally.
- **2013:** When Nelson Mandela turned 95 in July, we took a look back at the life and legacy of the beloved anti-apartheid leader and first black president of South Africa. At the time, Mandela had been hospitalized in Pretoria for a recurring lung infection, and was placed on life support after his condition deteriorated. Released in September after a three-month stay, he died at his home in Johannesburg on December 5.

- **2013:** Edward J. Snowden, a former contractor for the National Security Agency, reveals that he leaked documents detailing mass-surveillance programs of the U.S. government. Snowden, 29, holes up in a Hong Kong hotel after fleeing the United States and in July will be granted temporary asylum in Russia

- **2014:** Narendra Damodardas Modi is the 14th and current Prime Minister of India, in office since 26 May 2014. Modi, a leader of the Bharatiya Janata Party, was the Chief Minister of Gujarat from 2001 to 2014 and is a Member of Parliament from Varanasi.
- **2015:** First International Yoga Day: The UN declared 21st June as the International Yoga Day this year. Prime Minister Narendra Modi specifically selected this date as it is the day of Summer Solstice (the beginning of the transitional phase to Dakshinayana), the longest day of the year in the Northern Hemisphere.

- **2016:** The Olympic Games finally come to South America in 2016, with Rio de Janeiro as the host city. Golf and rugby sevens are new sports for 2016, and there will be a total 306 gold medals at stake.
- **2017:** The year 2017 was significant for the implementation of the Goods and Services Tax (GST) on 1st July, which replaced the complex web of indirect taxes with a unified tax structure across the country. Politically, the BJP won major state elections, including Uttar Pradesh, strengthening its national dominance. India also launched the South Asia Satellite, showcasing regional cooperation and technological advancement. This year marked deeper economic reform and digital push under the "Digital India" mission.
- **2018:** In 2018, the Indian judiciary and society witnessed transformative moments. The Supreme Court decriminalized Section 377, legalizing homosexuality and upholding LGBTQ+ rights. It also struck down the ban on women entering Sabarimala Temple, sparking nationwide debates on tradition versus gender equality. India also faced severe floods in Kerala, one of the worst in nearly a century, testing disaster response and unity. Politically, Congress gained ground by winning three major state elections-Rajasthan, Madhya Pradesh, and Chhattisgarh.

- **2019:** 2019 was a landmark year as Prime Minister Narendra Modi led the BJP to a landslide victory in the general elections, securing a second consecutive term. The most historic move came on 5th August, with the abrogation of Article 370, revoking Jammu and Kashmir's special status and bifurcating it into two Union Territories. The year also saw the passing of the Citizenship Amendment Act (CAA), which sparked widespread protests across India. On the global stage, India conducted the Balakot airstrikes in retaliation to the Pulwama attack, marking a significant military assertion.
- **2020:** The year 2020 was dominated by the outbreak of the COVID-19 pandemic, leading to a nationwide lockdown beginning on 25th March-one of the world's largest. The healthcare system was tested, and the migrant worker crisis exposed vulnerabilities in urban-rural dynamics. Despite the crisis, India made a strong diplomatic and manufacturing push through "Vaccine Maitri," supplying COVID-19 vaccines to several countries. The year also saw India-China border clashes in Galwan Valley, resulting in casualties and heightened geopolitical tensions.
- **2021:** In 2021, India ramped up its COVID-19 vaccination campaign, administering over a billion doses by the end of the year. The prolonged farmers' protest against three controversial agricultural laws dominated the political landscape, culminating in the repeal of the farm laws by the government in November.

  India also experienced a devastating second wave of COVID-19 in April-May, which caused immense strain on the healthcare infrastructure. The Tokyo Olympics saw India's best-ever medal haul, including a historic gold in javelin by Neeraj Chopra.
- **2023:** India made space history in 2023 with the successful Chandrayaan-3 mission, becoming the first country to land near the Moon's south pole, boosting its global reputation in space science. The G20 Presidency was held by India, hosting the G20 Summit in New Delhi and promoting themes of sustainability, multilateralism, and digital innovation. On the

economic front, India emerged as the fifth-largest economy, surpassing the UK in nominal GDP. Politically, preparations for the 2024 general elections began shaping national discourse.

- **2024:** In 2024, India held its general elections, and Narendra Modi secured a third consecutive term as Prime Minister, a rare political achievement in Indian history. The elections were notable for high voter turnout, significant youth participation, and debates around economy, governance, and nationalism. India continued to advance in digital infrastructure and AI policy, while also enhancing its strategic position in global geopolitics.
- **2025 (So far):** By mid-2025, India remains focused on implementing long-term economic reforms, digital innovation, and climate action. The government is working on new education and health initiatives, while diplomatic efforts have strengthened India's voice on platforms like the UN, BRICS, and Indo-Pacific dialogues. Tensions remain in regions like Ladakh and Northeast, but infrastructure, defense modernization, and environmental sustainability dominate national priorities. India also prepares to host several major international summits by the end of the year.

WORLD HISTORY TIMELINE

Ancient History

4.5 Billion - 1 B.C.

- **4.5 billion B.C.** Planet Earth forms.
- **3 billion B.C.** First signs of primeval life (bacteria and blue-green algae) appear in oceans.
- **600 million B.C.** Earliest date to which fossils can be traced.
- **2.5 million B.C.** First brain expansion; is believed to have used stone tools.
- **100,000 B.C.** First modern Homo sapiens in South Mrica.
- **70,000 B.C.** Neanderthal man uses fire and advanced tools.

- **35,000 B.C.** Neanderthal man replaces by later groups of Homosapiens
- **18,000 B.C.** Cro-Magnons replaces by later cultures.
- **10,000 B.C.** Semi-permanent agricultural settlements in Old World.
- **10,000-4,000 B.C.** Development of settlements into cities and development of skills such as the wheel, pottery, and improved methods of cultivation in Mesopotamia and elsewhere.
- **5500-3000 B.C.** Predynastic Egyptian cultures developed (5500-3100 B.C.). Men began using agriculture (c. 5000 B.C.). Earliest known civilization arose in Swner (4500-4000 B.C.). First year of Jewish calendar (3760 B.C.). First phonetic writing appears (c. 3500 B.C.). Sumerians develop a city state civilization (c. 3000 B.C.). Copper used by Egyptians and Sumerians.
- **3000-2000 B.C.** Pharaonic rule began in Egypt. King Khufu (Cheops). Construction of the Great Pyramid at Giza completed (2680 B.C.). The Great Sphirn:of Giza completed (2540 B.C.) by King Khafre.
- **3000-1500 B.C.** The most ancient civilization on the Indian subcontinent, the sophisticated and extensive Indus Valley civilization, flourished in what is today Pakistan. In Britain, Stonehenge erected according to some unknown astronomical rationale.
- **1000-900 B.C.** Solomon succeeds King David, builds Jerusalem temple. After Solomon's death, kingdom divided into Israel and Judah. Hebrew elders begin to write Old Testament books of Bible. Phoenicians colonize Spain with settlement at Cadiz.

- **900-800 B.C.** Phoenicians establish Carthage (c. 810 B.C.). The Iliad and the Odyssey, perhaps composed by Greek poet Homer.
- **800-700 B.C.** Prophets Amos, Hosea, Isaiah. First recorded Olympic games (776 B.C.). Legwdary founding of Rome by Romulus (753 B.C.). Assyrian king Sargon II conquers Hittites, Chaldeans, Samaria (end of Kingdom of Israel). Earliest written music. Chariots introduced into Italy by Etruscans.
- **700-600 B.C.** End of Assyrian Empire (616 B.C.). Founding of Byzantium by Greeks (c. 660 B.C.). Building of the Acropolis in Athens. Solon, Greek lawgiver (640-560 B.C.). Sappho of Lesbos, Greek poet (fl. c. 610-580 B.C.).
- **600-500 B.C.** Babylonian King Nebuchadnezzar builds empire, destroys Jerusalem (586 B.C.). Babylonian Captivity of the Jews (starting 587 B.C.). Cyrus the Great of Persia creates great empire, conquers Babylon (539 B.C.), and frees the Jews. Athenian democracy develops. Buddha (563-483 B.C.) founds Buddhism in India.
- **200-151 B.C.** Romans defeat Seleucid King Antiochus III at Thermopylae (191 B.C.)

- **150-101 B.C.** Third Punic War (149-146 B.C.): Rome destroys Carthage, killing 450,000 and enslaving the remaining 50,000 inhabitants.
- **100-51 B.C.** Julius Caesar (100-44 B.C.) invades Britain (55 B.C.) and conquers Gaul (France) (c. 50 B.C.). Romans conquer Seleucid Empire. Cleopatra on Egyptian throne (51-31 B.C.). Chinese develop use of paper (c. 100 B. C.).

- **50-1 B.C.** Caesar crosses Rubicon to fight Pompey (50 B.C.). Herod made Roman governor of Jud (37 B. C.).

1-999 (A.D.)

- **1-49:** Birth of Jesus Christ (variously given from 4 B.C. to AD. 7).
- **50-99:** Claudius poisoned (AD. 54), succeeded by Nero (commits suicide, AD. 68). Jews rev against Rome; Jerusalem destroyed (AD. 70). Roman persecutions of Christians begin (AD. 64 Colosseum built in Rome (AD. 71-80). First Gospels of St. Mark, St. John, St. Matthew.
- **100-149:** Hadrian rules Rome (AD. 117-138).
- **150-199:** Marcus Aurelius rules Rome (AD. 161-180). Oldest Mayan temples in Central America (AD. 200).
- **250-299:** Increasing invasions of the Roman Empire by Franks and Goths. Buddhism spreads in China. 300-349 Constantine the Great (rules AD. 312-337) reunites eastern and western Roman empires. First Gupta dynasty in India (c. AD. 320).
- **400-449:** Western Roman Empire disintegrates under weak emperors. St. Patrick returns to Ireland (AD. 432) and brings Christianity to the island. St. Augustine's City of God (AD. 411).
- **450-499:** Vandals destroy Rome (AD. 455). Western Roman Empire ends as Odoacer, German chieftain, overthrows last Roman emperor, Romulus Augustulus, and becomes king of Italy (A.D. 476). 500-549 Eastern and western churches reconcile (519).

- **550-599:** Beginnings of European silk industry. Mohammed, founder of Islam (570-632). Buddhism in Japan (c. 560). St. Augustine of Canterbury brings Christianity to Britain (597).
- **600-649:** Mohammed flees from Mecca-to Medina (the Hegira); first year of the Muslim calendar (622). Arabs conquer Jerusalem (637), conquer Persians (641).

- **650-699:** Arabs attack North Mrica (670), destroy Carthage (697).
- **700-749:** Arab Empire extends from Lisbon to China (by 716).
- **750-799:** Caliph Harun al-Rashid rules Arab empire (786-809) the 'golden age' of Arab culture. Vikings begin attacks on Britain (790), land in Ireland (795). City of Machu Picchu flourishes in Peru.
- **800-849:** Charlemagne crowned first Holy Roman Emperor in Rome (800). Charlemagne dies (814), succeeded by his son, Louis the Pious.
- **850-899:** Norsemen attack as far south as the Mediterranean but are thwarted (859), discover Iceland (861). Alfred the Great becomes king of Britain (871), defeats Danish invaders (878).

- **900-949:** Beginning of Mayan Post-Classical period (900-1519) Vikings discover Greenland (c. 900).
- **950-999:** Mieczyslaw I becomes first ruler of Poland (960). Eric the Red establishes first Viking colony in Greenland (982). Hugh Capet elected King of France in 987.

1000-1099 (A.D.)

- **1000-1300:** Classic Pueblo period of Anasazi culture.
- **1009:** Muslims destroy Holy Sepulchre in Jerusalem.
- **1013:** Danes control England.
- **1054:** Final separation between Eastern (Orthodox) and Western (Roman) churches.
- **1068:** Construction on the cathedral in Pisa, Italy, begins.
- **1095:** At Council of Clermont, Pope Urban II calls for a holy war to wrest control ofJerusalem from Muslims, which launches the First Crusade (1096), one of at least 8 European military campaigns between 1095 and 1291 to regain the Holy Land.

1100-1199 (A.D.)

- **1100-1300:**Construction of Cathedral at Chartres, France.
- **1144:** Second Crusade begins.

- **1150-1167:**Universities of Paris and Oxford founded in France and England.

1200-1299 (A.D.)

- **1211:** Genghis Khan invades China.
- **1241:** Mongols defeat Germars in Silesia, invade Poland and Hungary, withdraw from Europe after Ughetai, Mongol leader, dies.
- **1251:** Kublai Khan governs China, becomes ruler of Mongols (1259), establishes Yuan dynasty in China (1280), invades Burma (1287), and dies (1294).
- **1271:** Marco Polo of Venice travels to China, in court of Kublai Khan (1275-1292), returns to Genoa (1295) and writes 1 Yavels.

1300-1399 (A.D.)

- **1325:** The beginning of the Renaissance in Italy. Peak of Muslim culture in Spain. Small cannon in use.
- **1337-1453:**Hundred Years' War-English and French kings fight for control of France.
- **1347-1351:**At least 25 million people die in Europe's 'Black Death' (bubonic plague).
- **1368:** Ming Dynasty begins in China.
- **1398:** Tamerlane, the Mongol conqueror, begins last great conquest-Delhi.

1400-1499 (A.D.)

- **1407:** Casa di San Giorgio, one of the first public banks, founded in Genoa.

- **1428:** Joan of Arc leads French against English, captured by Burgundians (1430) and turned over to the English, burned at the stake as a witch after ecclesiastical trial (1431).
- **1450:** FlorencebecomescentreofRenaissance arts and learning.
- **1455:** The Wars of the Roses, civil wars between rival noble factions, begin in England (to 1485).

Having invented printing with movable type at Mainz, Germany, Johann Gutenberg completes first Bible.

1500-1599 (A.D.)

- **1501:** First black slaves in America brought to Spanish colony of Santo Domingo.
- **1503:** Leonardo da Vinci paints the Mona Lisa. Michelangelo sculpts the David (1504).
- **1517:** Turks conquer Egypt, control Arabia. Martin Luther postshis 95 theses denouncing church abuses on church door in Wittenberg—start of the Reformation in Germany.
- **1527:** Troops of the Holy Roman Empire attack Rome, imprison Pope Clement VII, the end of Italian Renaissance.
- **1535:** Reformation begins as Henry VIII makes himself head of English Church after being excommunicated by Pope.

- **1543:** Publication of On the Revolution of Heavenly Bodies by Polish scholar Nicolaus Copernicus gave his theory that the earth revolves around the sun.
- **1547:** Ivan IV ("the Terrible") crowned as Czar of Russia.
- **1553:** Roman Catholicism restored in England by Queen Mary 1.
- **1556:** Akbarthe Greatbecomes Mogulemperorof India.
- **1558:** Queen Elizabeth I ascends the throne (rules till 1603).
- **1580:** Francis Drake returns to England after circumnavigating the globe; knighted by Queen Elizabeth I (1581).
- **1582:** Pope Gregory XIII implements the Gregorian calendar.

1600-1699 (A.D.)

- **1600:** English East India Company established.
- **1610:** Galileo sees the moons of Jupiter through his telescope.

- **1614:** John Napier discovers logarithms.
- **1618:** Start of the Thirty Years' War.
- **1619:** A Dutch ship brings the first Mrican slaves to British North America.
- **1623:** New Netherland founded by Dutch West India Company.
- **1643:** Taj Mahal completed.

- **1644:** End of Ming Dynasty in China—Manchus come to power.
- **1648:** End of the Thirty Years' War.
- **1660:** English Parliament calls for the restoration of the monarchy; invites Charles II to return from France.
- **1661:** Charles II is crowned King of England. Louis XIV begins personal rule as absolute monarch.
- **1664:** British take New Amsterdam from the Dutch.
- **1665:** Great Plague in London kills 75,000.
- **1667:** Milton's Paradise Lost widely considered the greatest epic poem in English.
- **1682:** Pennsylvania founded by William Penn.

1700-1799 (A.D.)

- **1707:** United Kingdom of Great Britain formed-England, Wales, and Scotland joined by parliamentary Act of Union.
- **1755:** Samuel Johnson's Dictionary first published.
- **1757:** Beginning of British Empire in India as Robert Clive, British commander, defeats Nawab of Bengal at Plassey.
- **1765:** James Watt invents the steam engine.
- **1773:** The Boston Tea Party.
- **1775:** The American Revolution begins.
- **1778:** Capt. James Cook discovers Hawaii. Franz Mesmer uses hypnotism.
- **1787:** The Constitution of the United States signed.
- **1789:** French Revolution begins with the storming of the Bastille.

- **1793:** Louis XVI and Marie Antoinette executed.
- **1796:** Napoleon Bonaparte, French general, defeats Austrians.
- **1798:** Napoleon extends French conquests to Rome and Egypt. U.S. Navy Department established.

1800-1899 (A.D.)

- **1800:** Napoleon conquers Italy, firmly establishes himself as First Consul in France.
- **1801:** Austria makes temporary peace with France.
- **1804:** Haiti declares independence from France. Napoleon victorious over Austrian and Russian forces at the Battle of Austerlitz.
- **1808:** French armies occupy Rome and Spain, extending Napoleon's empire. Britain begins aiding Spanish guerrillas against Napoleon in Peninsular War.
- **1812:** Napoleon's Grand Army invades Russia in June. Forced to retreat in winter, most of Napoleon's 600,000 men are lost.
- **1814:** French defeated by allies (Britain, Austria, Russia, Prussia, Sweden, and Portugal) in War of Liberation. Napoleon exiled to Elba, off Italian coast.
- **1815:** Napoleon returns, 'Hundred Days' begin. Napoleon defeated by Wellington at Waterloo, banished again to St. Helena in South Atlantic.
- **1825:** First passenger-carrying railroad in England.
- **1826:** Joseph-Nicephore Niepcetakes the world's first photograph.
- **1833:** Slavery abolished in British Empire.

- **1834:** Charles Babbage invents analytical engine.
- **1837:** Victoria becomes queen of Great Britain.
- **1839:** First Opium War (to 1842) between Britain and China, over importation of drug into China.
- **1848:** Karl Marx and Friedrich Engels's 'Communist Manifesto'.
- **1849:** California gold rush begins.

- **1853:** Crimean War begins as Turkey declares war on Russia.
- **1861:** U.S. Civil War begins as attempts at compromise fail.
- **1866:** Alfred Nobel invents dynamite (patented in Britain, 1867).
- **1870:** Franco-Prussian War (to 1871) Napoleon III capitulates at Sedan.
- **1879:** Thomas A. Edison invents practical electric light.

- **1880:** U.S.-China treaty allows U.S. to restrict immigration of Chinese labor.
- **1885:** World's first skyscraper built in Chicago.
- **1886:** Statue of Liberty dedicated.
- **1893:** New Zealand becomes first country in the world to grant women the vote.
- **1895:** X-rays discovered by German physicist Wilhelm Roentgen.
- **1898:** Spanish-American War begins. Pierre and Marie Curie discover radium and polonium.
- **1899:** Boer War.

1900 - 2000

- **1901:** Queen Victoria dies, and is succeeded by her son, Edward VII.
- **1905:** The Russian Revolution of 1905 begins on 'Bloody Sunday'
- **1906:** San Francisco earthquake and three-day fire; more than 500 dead.
- **1911:** First use of aircraft as offensive weapon in Turkish-Italian War.
- **1912:** Titanic sinks on maiden voyage; over 1,500 drown.
- **1914:** World War I begins. Panama Canal officially opened.
- **1917:** First U.S. combat troops in France as U.S. declares war on Germany (April 6)
- **1918:** World War I ends.

- **1919:** Mahatma Gandhi initiates Satyagraha ('truth force') campaigns, beginninghis nonviolent resistance movement against British rule in India.
- **1920:** League of Nations holds first meeting at Geneva, Switzerland.

- **1923:** Adolf Hitler's "Beer Hall Putsch" in Munich fails.
- **1933:** Hitler appointed German chancellor, gets dictatorial powers.
- **1939:** World War II begins.
- **1940:** Churchill becomes Britain's prime minister.
- **1942:** Declaration of United Nations signed in Washington (Jan. 1).
- **1943:** Churchill and Roosevelt hold Casablanca Conference.
- **1945:** Hitler commits suicide. World War II ends.
- **1947:** India and Pakistan gain independence from Britain.
- **1948:** Gandhi assassinated in New Delhi by a Hindu fanatic.
- **1949:** Start of North Atlantic Treaty Organization (NATO)-treaty signed by 12 nations. Korean War begins.
- **1951:** Colour television introduced in U.S. Libya gains independence.

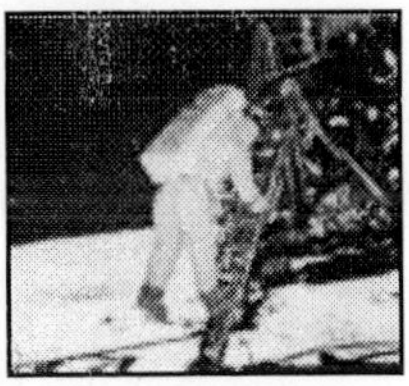

- **1957:** Russians launch Sputnik 1, first Earth—orbiting satellite-the Space Age begins.
- **1961:** Moscow announces putting first man in orbit around Earth, Maj. Yuri A. Gagarin.
- **1968:** Apollo 11 astronauts-Neil A. Armstrong, Edwin E. Aldrin, Jr., and Michael Collins-take man's first walk on moon (July 20).
- **1977:** First woman Episcopal priest ordained (Jan. 1).
- **1981:** AIDS is first identified.
- **1984:** Indian prime minister Indira Gandhi assassinated by two Sikh bodyguards; 1,000 killed in anti-Sikh riots; son Rajiv succeeds her.
- **1988:** Benazir Bhutto, first Islamic woman prime minister, chosen to lead Pakistan.

- 1989: Dalai Lama wins Nobel Peace Prize.
- **1990:** World Wide Web debuts, popularizes Internet.
- **1992:** Bill Clinton elected president of US.
- **1993:** President of Sri Lanka assassinated.
- **1994:** Four convicted in World Trade Center bombing. Small plane crashes into White House.
- **1996:** Kofi Annan named UN secretary-general.

- **1999:** Military coup led by Gen. Pervez Musharraf overthrows Pakistani government. China launches first spacecraft.

2001 to Present

- **2001:** Terrorists attack United States. Hijackers ram jetliners into twin towers of New York City's World Trade Center and the Pentagon. A fourth hijacked plane crashes 80 mts outside of Pittsburgh. Toll of dead is more than 3,000. Within days, Islamic militant Osama bin Laden and the al-Qaeda terrorist network are identified as the parties behind the attacks (Sept. 11). 9/11 attacks destroy the World Trade Center in New York. Afghan War begins. Wikipedia founded. President Joseph Estrada of the Philippines impeached.
- **2003:** International Atomic Energy Agency (IAEA) discovers Iran's concealed nuclear activities and calls for intensified inspections (June 18). Saddam Hussein is captured by American troops (Dec. 13). 2003 Invasion of Iraq begins.
- **2007:** Anti-government protests in Myanmar crushed by ruling junta. Great Recession begins.
- **2009:** Gaza War ends; Gaza blockade continues. Election protests begin in Iran. Second Chechen War ends. Burj Khalifa in Dubai, the world's tallest skyscraper, is completed. Great Recession officially

ends. Former President Corazon Aquino of the Philippines dies due to colon cancer.

- **2010:** August – The World Health Organization declares the H1N1 influenza pandemic over, saying worldwide flu activity has returned to typical seasonal patterns.
- **2010:** October - XIX Commonwealth Games, were held in New Delhi, India, from 3 to 14 October 2010.
- **2010:** October – An earthquake and consequent tsunami off the coast of Sumatra, Indonesia, kills over 400 people and leave hundreds missing.
- **2010:** November 11–12 – The G-20 summit is held in Seoul, South Korea. Korea becomes the first non-G8 nation to host a G-20 leaders summit.
- **2011:** March 11 – A 9.0 magnitude earthquake and subsequent tsunami hits the east Japan causing over 13,000 deaths with another 15,000 missing. Tsunami warnings are issued in 50 countries and territories. Emergencies are declared at four nuclear power plants affected by the quake.
- **2012:** Oct. 9 In Pakistan, Taliban members shoot 14-year-old Malala Yousafzai in the head and neck. The shooting occurs while Yousafzai is on her way home on a school bus filled with children. She was targeted for her outspokenness against the Taliban and her determination to get an education.
- **2013:** Pope Benedict XVIunexpectedlyannouncedhisresignation on grounds of poor health, making him the first pope to do so in nearly 600 years. Cardinal Jorge Mario Bergoglio from Argentina was subsequently elected as Pope Francis.
- **2014:** Malaysia Airlines Flight 370 (MH370/MAS370)[a] was a scheduled international passenger flight operated by Malaysia Airlines that disappeared on 8 March 2014 while flying from Kuala Lumpur International Airport, Malaysia, to Beijing Capital International Airport in China. The aircraft last made voice contact with air traffic control at 01:19 MYT, 8 March (17:19 UTC, 7 March) when it was over the South China Sea, less than an hour after takeoff. It disappeared from air traffic controllers' radar screens.

- **2015:** Greece misses a key debt repayment deadline to the IMF, as Grexit becomes part of the media lexicon and Greeks at home and abroad being to panic about their own finances. The "Greek crisis" dominates the headlines.
- **2016:** Juno is a NASA space probe orbiting the planet Jupiter after entering orbit on July 5, 2016, the prelude to 20 months of scientific data collection to be followed by a planned deorbit. It was launched from Cape Canaveral Air Force Station on August 5, 2011, as part of the New Frontiers program and ranged into Jupiter's orbit on July 4, 2016.

- **2017 :** Donald Trump withdraws the U.S. from the Paris Climate Accord. North Korea conducts multiple missile tests, increasing global tensions. MeToo movement gains global momentum after Harvey Weinstein allegations. Rohingya refugee crisis escalates as thousands flee Myanmar to Bangladesh. UK triggers Article 50, officially beginning Brexit process. French President Emmanuel Macron elected, defeating far-right Marine Le Pen.
- **2018 :** U.S.-North Korea summit held in Singapore (June), the first between leaders of both nations. Yellow Vest protests erupt in France against fuel tax hikes and economic inequality. Jamal Khashoggi murdered in Saudi consulate in Istanbul, causing global outrage. California wildfires become the deadliest and most destructive in state history. Ethiopia and Eritrea end decades-long war, signing peace deal. Data privacy concerns rise after Facebook-Cambridge Analytica scandal.
- **2019 :** Notre-Dame Cathedral in Paris severely damaged by fire (April). Amazon Rainforest fires attract global attention and concern over deforestation. Hong Kong protests begin over extradition law, evolve into democracy movement. Greta Thunberg leads global climate strikes, becoming a symbol for youth activism. India revokes Article 370, removing special status of Jammu and Kashmir. COVID-19 first reported in Wuhan, China (December).

- **2020 :** OVID-19 pandemic causes global lockdowns, economic crises, and millions of deaths. Black Lives Matter protests erupt globally after the murder of George Floyd. Beirut explosion (August 4) kills over 200, caused by ammonium nitrate storage. Joe Biden elected U.S. President, defeating Donald Trump (November 3). U.K. officially exits the EU (January 31, Brexit completion). Nagorno-Karabakh war erupts between Armenia and Azerbaijan.
- **2021 :** Global COVID-19 vaccination campaigns begin, led by Pfizer, Moderna, and others. Capitol Hill riots in Washington, D.C., as pro-Trump supporters storm U.S. Capitol (January 6). Taliban retake Afghanistan after U.S. troop withdrawal; Kabul falls (August). Ever Given cargo ship blocks the Suez Canal, disrupting global trade (March). Israel-Palestine conflict flares up in Gaza; over 250 killed in 11-day conflict. UN Climate Change Conference (COP26) held in Glasgow to strengthen Paris commitments.
- **2022:** Russia invades Ukraine (February 24), triggering global crisis, sanctions, and war. Queen Elizabeth II dies (September 8) after 70 years on the throne; Charles III becomes king. Sri Lanka economic collapse leads to protests and resignation of President Rajapaksa. Mahsa Amini protests begin in Iran after her death in morality police custody. Monkeypox outbreak declared global health emergency by WHO. FIFA World Cup held in Qatar; Argentina wins with Lionel Messi starring.
- **2023 :** Earthquakes in Turkey and Syria kill over 50,000 people (February). Narges Mohammadi awarded Nobel Peace Prize for her advocacy for women's rights in Iran. AI boom continues as ChatGPT and generative AI become widely used globally. Mass unrest in Israel over judicial reforms sparks protests. China-U.S. tensions escalate over Taiwan and surveillance balloons. Barbie and Oppenheimer films dominate global cinema, becoming cultural events.
- **2024 :** Nihon Hidankyo wins Nobel Peace Prize, honoring atomic bomb survivors and disarmament efforts. India holds general elections, Narendra Modi wins third consecutive term. Global climate events worsen, with severe wildfires in Canada, Australia, and Mediterranean. U.S. Presidential campaign begins, with Trump and Biden running

again. AI regulations introduced in the EU and discussed at global forums. Russia-Ukraine war continues, with new escalations and international tensions. Israel-Hamas conflict escalates again, drawing worldwide concern.

- **2025 (events till mid-year):** U.S. presidential inauguration expected January 2025. Global debates on AI governance and ethics intensify. United Nations Climate Pact (post-Paris Agreement) expected to be signed. Economic recovery plans from COVID-19 aftermath continue in many nations. South China Sea tensions increase, involving U.S., China, and ASEAN nations. Ongoing protests in Iran, Belarus, and Russia for democratic rights. Continued humanitarian crises in Sudan, Gaza, Myanmar, and parts of Africa.
- **United Nations General Assembly 2025 (September 2025):** World leaders are expected to convene at the annual session of the United Nations General Assembly in New York, with high-level discussions on global security, AI regulation, climate finance, and post-pandemic economic resilience amid rising geopolitical tensions.
- **COP30 Global Climate Summit (November 2025):** The COP30 climate conference is expected to take place in Brazil, focusing on emissions reduction targets, climate adaptation funding, and progress on commitments made under the Paris Agreement, particularly for developing and climate-vulnerable nations.

From 1947-1950

Name	Began	Ended
Louis Mountbatten 'Earl Mountbatten of Burma'	August 15, 1947	June 21, 1948
Chakravarthi Rajagopalachari	June 21, 1948	January 26,1950

LIST OF NOBEL PEACE PRIZE WINNERS 2015-2025

Year	Name
2015	Tunisian National Dialogue Quartet
2016	Juan Manuel Santos (Colombia)

2017 International Campaign to Abolish Nuclear Weapons (ICAN, Switzerland)

2018 Denis Mukwege (DR Congo) & Nadia Murad (Iraq)

Denis Mukwege (DR Congo) & Nadia Murad (Iraq)

2019 Abiy Ahmed (Ethiopia)

2020 World Food Programme (United Nations)

2021 Maria Ressa (Philippines) & Dmitry Muratov (Russia)

Nihon Hidankyo

2022 Ales Bialiatski

2023 Narges Mohammadi

2024 Nihon Hidankyo

2025 María Corina Machado (Venezuela)

❑❑❑

The Earth – Quick Facts

5

The Earth is one of the most fascinating of all planets. It is the home of human beings and other living things. The earth is a sphere covered with rock, water, soil and air. It is just the right distance away from the sun. We all need sunlight and warmth for life. If the earth was too close, it would be too hot for living things and if it were too far, it would be too cold. Also, water is a key element for all living things, and the earth has plenty.

The earth is the fifth largest planet and the third planet from the sun. Its diameter is 8,000 miles long. The earth is about 93 million miles from the sun. The atmosphere of Earth contains enough oxygen to sustain life. This can be compared to with other planets such as Mars, where it consists of only carbon dioxide.

- Surface Area of the Planet (510,066,000 sq km)
- Land Area on the Planet (148,647,000 sq km) 29.1%
- Ocean Area (335,258,000 sq km)
- Total Water Area (361,419,000 sq km) 70.9%
- Type of Water (97% salt), (3% fresh)
- (To convert sq km (kilometers) to sq miles, multiply kilometers by: 0.386102)
- Estimated Weight (mass) (5,940,000,000,000,000,000,000 metric tons)
- Estimated Age 4.6 billion years
- Current Population 5,446,131,714
- Surface Area (510,066,000 sq km) Land Area
- (148,647,000 sq km) 29.1% Ocean Area (335,258,000 sq km)

7 continents map with 5 oceans

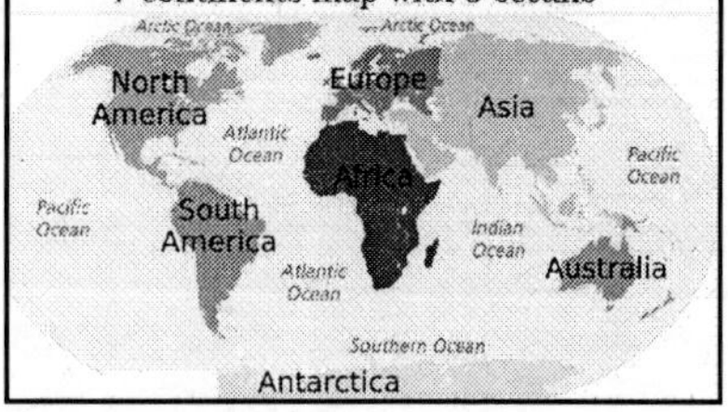

- The earth orbits the Sun at (66,700 mph), (107,320 km per hour)
- SUN ORBIT The earth orbits the Sun every 365 days, 5 hours, 48 minutes and 46 seconds
- ONE DAY: 23 hours, 56 minutes, 4.09 seconds (We round this to 24 hours)
- ONE YEAR: 365 days, 6 hours, 9 minutes, 9.54 seconds (We round this to 365 days)
- NATURAL SATELLITES: 1
- DISTINCTIVE FEATURE: (One of the) Only planet that supports life.

CONTINENTS OF THE EARTH

The seven continents are Asia, Australia, Africa, Antarctica, North America, South America and Europe. It is seen that each continent has a special shape. Some of these continents are connected while the water separates others.

Continents (by size)

1. Asia - (44,579,000 sq km)
2. Africa - (30,065,000 sq km)
3. North America - (24,256,000 sq km)
4. South America - (17,819,000 sq km)
5. Antarctica - (13,209,000 sq km)
6. Europe - (9,938,000 sq km)
7. Australia/Oceania - (7,687,000 sq km)

Continents (by population)

1. Asia - (3,674,000,000)
2. Africa - (778,000,000)
3. Europe - (732,000,000)
4. North America - (483,000,000)
5. South America - (342,000,000)
6. Australia/Oceania - (31,000,000)
7. Antarctica - (0)

Continents (by the number of countries)

1. Africa - (53)
2. Europe - (46)
3. Asia - (44)
4. North America - (23)
5. Oceania - (14)
6. South America - (12)

LIST OF COUNTRIES

Country	Capital	Official Language(s)
A		
Abkhazia	Sukhumi Abkhaz	Abkhaz(Cyrillic alphabet) Russian (Cyrillic alphabet)
Afghanistan	Kabul	Pashtu (Afghan), Dari (Persian)
Albania	Tirana	(Arabic script)Albanian
Algeria	Algiers	Arabic(Arabic script)
Åland Islands	Mariehamn	Swedish
American Samoa	Pago Pago	SamoanEnglish
Angola	Luanda	Portuguese
Anguilla	The Valley	English
Antigua and Barbuda	Saint John's	English
Argentina	Buenos Aires	Spanish
Armenia	Yerevan	Armenian
Aruba	Oranjestad	(Armenian alphabet)Dutch
Australia	Canberra	English
Austria	Vienna	German
Azerbaijan	Baku	Azeri(Cyrillic alphabet)
B		
Bahamas	Nassau	English
Bahrain	Manama Arabic	Arabic
Bangladesh	Dhaka	(Arabic script)Bengali (Bengali script)
Barbados	Bridgetown	English

Australia

Belarus	Minsk	Belarusian (Cyrillic alphabet) (Latin Belarusian Alphabet) Russian (Cyrillic alphabet)
Belgium	Brussels	Dutch, French, German
Belize	Belmopan	English
Benin	Porto-Novo	French
Bermuda	Hamilton	English
Bhutan	Thimphu	Dzongkha
Bolivia	La Paz	Spanish
Bosnia-Herzegovina	Sarajevo	Bosnian, Serbian, Croatian (Cyrillic alphabet)
Botswana	Gaborone	English
Brazil	Brasilia	Portuguese
British Virgin Islands	Road Town	English
Brunei	Bandar Seri	Malay Begawan (Jawi script)
Bulgaria	Sofia	Bulgarian (Cyrillic alphabet)
Burkina Faso	Ouagadougou	French
Burundi	Bujumbura	Kirundi

C

Cambodia	Phnom Penh	Cambodian
Cameroon	Yaounde	French, English
Canada	Ottawa	English, French
Cape Verde	Praia	Portuguese Cayman Islands George Town English Central African Republic Bangui French Chad N'Djamena French
Chile	Santiago	Spanish
China	Beijing	Chinese (Jiantizi) Christmas Island The Settlement English
Cocos Islands	West Island	English
Colombia	Bogotá	Spanish
Comoros	Moroni	Shikomor, Arabic (Arabic script), French
Congo-Brazzaville	Brazzaville	French
Congo-Kinshasa	Kinshasa	French

Cook Islands	Avarua	English
Costa Rica	San José	Spanish
Côte d'Ivoire	Yamoussoukro	French
Croatia	Zagreb	Croatian
Cuba	Havana	Spanish
Cyprus	Nicosia	Greek (Greek alphabet) Turkish
Czech Republic	Prague	Czech

D

Denmark	Copenhagen	Danish
Djibouti	Djibouti	Arabic (Arabic script) French
Dominica	Roseau	English
Dominican Republic	Santo Domingo	Spanish

E

East Timor	Díli	Tetum, Portuguese
Ecuador	Quito	Spanish
Egypt	Cairo	Arabic (Arabic script)
El Salvador	San Salvador	Spanish
Equatorial Guinea	Malabo	Spanish
Eritrea	Asmara	Tigrignan, Arabic
Estonia	Tallinn	Estonian
Ethiopia	Addis Ababa	Amharic

F

Falkland Islands	Port Stanley	English
Faroe Islands	Tórshavn	Faroese
Fiji	Suva	English, Fijian, Hindustani
Finland	Helsinki	Finnish, Swedish
France	Paris	French
French Guiana	Cayenne	French
French Polynesia	Papeete	French

G

Gabon	Libreville	French
Gambia	Banjul	English
Georgia	T'bilisi	Georgian (Georgian alphabet)

Germany	Berlin	German
Ghana	Accra	English
Gibraltar	Accra	English
Greece	Athens	Greek (Greek alphabet)
Greenland	Nuuk	Greenlandic, Danish
Grenada	Saint George's	English
Guadeloupe	Basse-Terre	French
Guam	Hagatna	English
Guatemala	Guatemala City	Spanish
Guernsey	St Peter Port	English
Guinea	Conakry	French
Guinea-Bissau	Bissau	Portuguese
Guyana	Georgetown	English

H

Haiti	Port-au-Prince	French
Honduras	Tegucigalpa	Spanish
Hong Kong	Victoria City	English, Cantonese (Hanzi)
Hungary	Budapest	Hungarian

I

Iceland	Reykjavik	None, Icelandic is de facto
India	New Delhi	English, Hindi (Devanagari script)
Indonesia	Jakarta	Indonesian
Iran	Tehran	Persian (Arabic script)
Iraq	Baghdad	Arabic (Arabic script)
Ireland	Dublin	Irish, English
Isle of Man	Douglas	English, Manx
Israel	Jerusalem	Hebrew (Hebrew alphabet) Arabic (Arabic script)
Italy	Rome	Italian

J

Jamaica	Kingston	English
Japan	Tokyo	Japanese (Kanji)
Jersey	Saint Helier	English, Jèrriais
Jordan	Amman	Arabic (Arabic script)

K		
Kazakhstan	Astana	Kazakh (Cyrillic alphabet)
Kenya	Nairobi	English, Swahili
Kiribati	South Tarawa	English, Gilbertese
Kosovo and Metohija	Priština	Serbian (Cyrillic alphabet) Albanian
Kuwait	Kuwait City	Arabic (Arabic script)
Kyrgyzstan	Bishkek	Kyrgyz, Russian Cyrillic alphabet
L		
Laos	Vientiane	Lao, Lao alphabet
Latvia	Riga	Latvian
Lebanon	Beirut	Arabic (Arabic script)
Lesotho	Maseru	Sesotho, English
Liberia	Monrovia	English
Libya	Tripoli	Arabic (Arabic script)
Liechtenstein	Vaduz	German
Lithuania	Vilnius	Lithuanian
Luxembourg	Luxembourg	Luxembourgian, German, French
M		
Macao Macedonia	Skopje	Portuguese, Cantonese (Hanzi) Macedonian (Cyrillic alphabet)
Madagascar	Antananarivo	Malagasy, French
Malawi	Lilongwe	English, Chichewa
Malaysia	Kuala Lumpur	Malay
Maldives	Malé	Dhivehi, Thaana script
Mali	Bamako	French
Malta	Valletta	Maltese
Marshall Islands	Dalap-Uliga-Darrit	English
Martinique	Fort-de-France	French
Mauritania	Nouakchott	French Arabic (Arabic script)
Mauritius	Port Louis	French
Mayotte	Mamoutzou	French
Mexico	Mexico City	Spanish
Micronesia	Palikir	English

Moldova	Chiºinãu	Moldovan (Romanian)
Monaco		French
Mongolia	Ulaanbaatar	Mongolian (Cyrillic alphabet)
Montserrat	Brades	Estate English
Morocco	Rabat	Arabic (Arabic script)
Mozambique	Maputo	Portuguese
Myanmar	Yangôn	Burmese

N

Nagorno-Karabakh	Stepanakert	Albanian (Albanian alphabet) Azeri (Cyrillic alphabet)
Namibia	Windhoek	English
Nauru	no capital	English, Nauruan
Nepal	Kathmandu	Nepali, Devanagari
Netherlands	Amsterdam	Dutch
Netherlands	Antilles	Willemstad Dutch
New Caledonia	Nouméa	French
New Zealand	Wellington	English, Maori
Nicaragua	Managua	Spanish
Niger	Niamey	French
Nigeria	Abuja	English
Niue	Alofi	Niuean, English
Norfolk	Island	Kingston English
North Korea	Pyongyang	Korean (Hangul)
Northern	Cyprus	Nicosia Turkish
Northern Mariana Islands	Saipan	English, Chamorro, Carolinian
Norway	Oslo	Norwegian (Bokmål & Nynorsk) Sami

O

Oman	Muscat	Arabic

P

Pakistan	Islamabad	Urdu, Arabic script
Palau	Koror	English, Palauan
Palestine	Gaza City	Arabic, Hebrew
Panama	Panama	City Spanish

Papua New Guinea	Port Moresby	English, Tok Pisin, Hiri Motu
Paraguay	Asuncion	Spanish
Peru	Lima	Spanish
Philippines	Manila	Filipino, English
Pitcairn Island	Adamstown	English
Poland	Warsaw	Polish, Ukrainian, German
Portugal	Lisbon	Portuguese
Puerto Rico	San Juan	Spanish, English
Puntland	Garowe	Somali
Q		
Qatar	Doha	Arabic
R		
Reunion	Saint-Denis	French
Romania	Bucharest	Romanian
Russia	Moscow	Russian (Cyrillic alphabet)
Rwanda	Kigali	French, Kinyarwanda, English
S		
Saint-Pierre and Miquelon French		Saint-Pierre
Saint Helena	Jamestown	English
Saint Kitts and Nevis	Basseterre	English
Saint Lucia	Castries	English
Saint Vincent and	Kingstown	English the Grenadines
Samoa	Apia	English
San Marino	San Marino	Italian
Sao Tome and Principe	Sao Tome	Portuguese
Saudi Arabia	Riyadh	Arabic (Arabic script)
Senegal	Dakar	
Serbia and Montenegro	Belgrade	
Seychelles	Port Victoria	Seychellois Creole, French, English
Sierra Leone	Freetown	English
Singapore	Malay	English, Chinese (Mandarin)
Slovakia	Bratislava	

Slovenia	Ljubljana	
Solomon Islands	Honiara	
Somalia	Mogadishu	
Somaliland	Hargeisa	
South Africa	Pretoria	English, Afrikaans, Zulu
South Korea	Seoul	Korean (Hangul)
South Ossetia	Tskhinvali	Ossetian (Cyrillic alphabet)
Spain	Madrid	Spanish
Sri Lanka	Colombo	
Sudan	Khartoum	Arabic (Arabic script)
Suriname	Paramaribo	Dutch
Svalbard	Longyearbyen	Norwegian
Swaziland	Mbabane	
Sweden	Stockholm	Swedish
Switzerland	Berne	German, French, Italian, Romansh
Syria	Damascus	

T

Taiwan	Taipei	Chinese (Hanzi)
Tajikistan	Dushanbe	
Tanzania	Dodoma	
Thailand	Bangkok	
Tibet	Lhasa	Tibetan
Togo	Lome	French
Tokelau		
Tonga	Nuku'alofa	
Transnistria	Tiraspol	Moldovan, Russian (Cyrillic alphabet)
Trinidad and Tobago	Port-of-Spain	English
Tunisia	Tunis	Arabic
Turkey	Ankara	
Turkmenistan	Ashgabat	
Turks and Caicos Islands	Cockburn Town	English
Tuvalu	Fongafale (in Funafuti)	

U

Uganda	Kampala	
Ukraine	Kiev	
United Arab Emirates	Abu Dhabi	Arabic
United Kingdom	London	None, English is de facto, Welsh,
Scots United States	Washington, D.C.	None, English is de facto, Spanish,
Cajun		
French		
Uruguay	Montevideo	Spanish
Uzbekistan	Tashkent	

V

Vanuatu	Port Vila	
Vatican City		Latin
Venezuela	Caracas	Spanish
Vietnam	Hanoi	
Virgin Islands	Charlotte Amalie	

W

Wallis and Futuna	Mata-Utu	French
Western Sahara	Laayoune	Arabic (Arabic script)

Y

Yemen	Sanaa	Arabic (Arabic script)

Z

Zambia	Lusaka	English
Zimbabwe	Harare	English

HOTTEST, COLDEST, DRIEST, AND WETTEST PLACES

- **Hottest Place**- Dalol, Denakil Depression, Ethiopi (l., annual average temperature (93.2°F, 34°C)
- **Coldest Place**- P1:lteau Station, Antarctica, annual average temperature (-567°C)
- **Wettest Place**- Mawsynram, Assam, India, annual average rainfall (11,873 nun, 467.4")

- **Driest Place**- Atacama Desert, Chile, imperceptible rainfall on a yearly basis

Driest Inhabited Places (Rainfall in inches per year)

- Aswan, Egypt 0.02"
- Luxor, Egypt 0.03"
- Africa Desert, Chile 0.04"
- lea, Peru 0.1"
- Antofagasta, Chile 0.2"
- El Minya, Egypt 0.2"
- Asyut, Egypt 0.2"

Wettest Inhabited Places (Rainfall in inches per year)

- Buenaventira, Colombia 267"
- Monrovia, Liberia 202"
- Pagp Pago, American Samoa 198"
- Moulein, Burma (Myanmar) 192"
- Lae, Papua New Guinea 183"
- Bagnio, Philippines 180"
- Sylhet, Bangladesh 178"

Oceans' Greatest Depths

- 1 Pacific Ocean (35,837 ft) (10,924 meters)
- 2 Atlantic Ocean (30,246 ft) (9,219 meters)
- 3 Indian Ocean (24,460 ft) (7,455 meters)
- 4 Caribbean Sea (22,788 ft) (6,946 meters)
- 5 Arctic Ocean (18,456 ft) (5,625 meters)
- 6 South China Sea (16,456 ft) (5,016 meters)
- 7 Bering Sea (15,659 ft) (4,773 meters)
- 8 Mediterranean Sea (15,197 ft) (4,632 meters)
- 9 Gulf of Mexico (12,425 ft) (3,787 meters)
- 10 Japan Sea (12,276 ft) (3,742 meters)

Note that official depths for the Southern Ocean are still disputed. Current measurements indicate its greatest depth to be 23,737 ft (7,236 meters). That would make it the third deepest body of water on the planet.

HIGHEST WATERFALLS OF THE WORLD

Name(s) (foreign)	Location	Source/River	Height	
			Feet	Meters
Angel (Salto Angel)	Canaima Nat'l Park,	Upper trib. of Rio	3,212	979
Tugela	Natal Nat'l Park,South	Tugela River	3,110	947
Utigord (Utigordsfoss)	Norway	Glacier fed	2,625	800
Monge (Mongefoss)	Marstein, Norway	Mongebeck	2,540	774
Gocta Cataracts	Chachapoyas, Peru		2,532	771
Yosemite	Yosemite Nat'lPark,	Yosemite Creek	2,425	739
Espelands (Espelandsfoss)	Hardanger Fjord, Norway	Opo River	2,307	703
Lower Mar Valley (Ostra Mardolafoss)	Eikesdal, Norway	Mardals Stream	2,151	6552
Tyssestrengene	Odda, Norway	Tyssa River	2,123	647
Cuquenan (SaltoKukenan)	Kukenan Tepuy, Venezuela	Cuquenan River	2,000	610
Dudhsagar	Goa/Karnataka,India	Khandepar River	1,969	600
Sutherland	Milford Sound, New Zealand	Arthur River	1,904	580
Kjell (Kjellfossen)	Gudvanger, Norway	Gudvangen Glacier	1,841	561
Takkakaw	Yoho Nat'l Park, B.C., Canada	Takkakaw Creek	1,650	503
Ribbon	Yosemite Nat'l Park, California,U.S.	Ribbon Stream	1,612	491
King George VI	Guyana	Courantyne River	1,600	488

Upper Mar Valley Mardalsfossen	nr. Eikesdal, Norway	Mardals Stream	1,536	468
Kaliuwaa (Sacred)	Pahu, Hawaii, U.S.	Kalanui Stream	1,520	463
Della	Strathcona Provincial Park,B.C., Canada	Della Lake	1,444	440
Gavarnie	nr. Lourdes, France	Gave de Pau	1,384	422
Cachoeira da Fumaça	Chapada Diamantia Nat'l Park, Brazil, (Glassor Smoke)	—	1,378	420
Giessbach	Bern, Switzerland	Giessbach River	1,312	400
Krimmler	Hohe Tauern Nat'l Park, Austria	Krimmler Ache	1,250	381
Vettis (Vettisfoss)	Jotunheimen, Norway	Utla (Trib.Mörkedola)	1,215	370
Papalaua	Molokai, Hawaii,U.S.	Kawai Nui Stream	1,200	366
Tin Mine	Kosciusko Nat'l Park, Australia	Tin Mine Creek	1,182	360
Silver Strand	Yosemite Nat'lPark,	Silver Strand Creek	1,170	357
Wallaman	nr. Ingham,Australia	Wallaman Creek	1,001	305
Spray Stream (Staubbachfalle)	Lauterburnnental, Switzerland	Staubbach Brook	984	300
King Edward VIII	Guyana	Courantyne	850	259
Gersoppa (Jog)	Western Ghats,India	Sharavati	830	253
Basaseachic (Salto Basaseachic)	Barance del Cobre, Mexico	Piedra Volada Creek	812	246
Waipio	Kauai, Hawaii, U.S.	Kekee Stream	800	244
Kaieteur	Guyana	Potaro, (trib. Rio Essequibo)	740	225
Kalambo	Tanzania/Zambia	Kalambo River	726	221
Wollomombi	nr. Armidale,Australia	Wollomombi	722	220
Feigum	Lusterfjord,Norway	Feigumelvi	715	218

HIGHEST MOUNTAIN PEAKS OF THE WORLD

Mountain Peak	Range	Location	Height	
			ft.	m
Everest	Himalayas	Nepal/Tibet	29,035	8,850
K2 (GodwinAusten)	Karakoram	Pakistan/China	28,250	8,611
Kanchenjunga	Himalayas	India/Nepal	28,169	8,586
Lhotse I	Himalayas	Nepal/Tibet	27,940	8,516
Makalu I	Himalayas	Nepal/Tibet	27,766	8,463
Cho Oyu	Himalayas	Nepal/Tibet	26,906	8,201
Dhaulagiri	Himalayas	Nepal	26,795	8,167
Nanga Parbat	Himalayas	Pakistan	26,660	8,125
Annapurna	Himalayas	Nepal	26,545	8,091
Broad Peak	Karakoram	Pakistan/China	26,400	8,047
Gasherbrum II	Karakoram	Pakistan/China	26,360	8,035
Shishma Pangma (Gosainthan)	Himalayas	Tibet	26,289	8,013
Annapurna II	Himalayas	Nepal	26,041	7,937
Gyachung Kang	Himalayas	Nepal	25,910	7,897
Disteghil Sar	Karakoram	Pakistan	25,858	7,882
Himalchuli	Himalayas	Nepal	25,801	7,864
Nuptse	Himalayas	Nepal	25,726	7,841
Nanda Devi	Himalayas	India	25,663	7,824
Masherbrum	Karakoram	Kashmir, India	25,660	7,821
Rakaposhi	Karakoram	Pakistan	25,551	7,788
Kanjut Sar	Karakoram	Pakistan	25,461	7,761
Kamet	Himalayas	India/Tibet	25,446	7,756
Namcha Barwa	Himalayas	Tibet	25,445	7,756
Gurla Mandhata	Himalayas	Tibet	25,355	7,728
Kungur	Muztagh Ata	China	25,325	7,719
Tirich Mir	Hindu Kush	Pakistan	25,230	7,690
Saser Kangri	Karakoram	India	25,172	7,672
Makalu II	Himalayas	Nepal	25,120	7,657
Kula Kangri	Himalayas	Bhutan	24,783	7,554
Chang-tzu	Himalayas	Tibet	24,780	7,553

Muztagh Ata	Muztagh Ata	China	24,757	7,546
Skyang	Himalayas	Kashmir	24,750	7,544
Ismail Samani Peak (formerly Communism Peak)	Pamirs	Tajikistan	24,590	7,495
Jongsong Peak	Himalayas	Nepal	24,472	7,459
Pobeda Peak	Tien Shan	Kyrgyzstan	24,406	7,439
Sia Kangri	Himalayas	Kashmir	24,350	7,422
Haramosh Peak	Karakoram	Pakistan	24,270	7,397
Istoro Nal	Hindu Kush	Pakistan	24,240	7,388
Tent Peak	Himalayas	Nepal	24,165	7,365
Chomo Lhari	Himalayas	Tibet/Bhutan	24,040	7,327
Chamlang	Himalayas	Nepal	24,012	7,319
Kabru	Himalayas	Nepal	24,002	7,316
Alung Gangri	Himalayas	Tibet	24,000	7,315
Baltoro Kangri	Himalayas	Kashmir	23,990	7,312
Muztagh Ata (K-5)	Kunlun	China	23,890	7,282
Mana	Himalayas	India	23,860	7,273
Baruntse	Himalayas	Nepal	23,688	7,220
Nepal Peak	Himalayas	Nepal	23,500	7,163
Amne Machin	Kunlun	China	23,490	7,160
Gauri Sankar	Himalayas	Nepal/Tibet	23,440	7,145
Badrinath	Himalayas	India	23,420	7,138
Nunkun	Himalayas	Kashmir	23,410	7,135
Pyramid	Himalayas	Nepal	23,400	7,132
Api	Himalayas	Nepal	23,399	7,132
Pauhunri	Himalayas	India/China	23,385	7,128
Trisul	Himalayas	India	23,360	7,120
Korzhenevski Peak	Pamirs	Tajikistan	23,310	7,105
Kangto	Himalayas	Tibet	23,260	7,090
Nyainqentanglha	NyainqentanglhaShan	China	23,255	7,088
Trisuli	Himalayas	India	23,210	7,074
Dunagiri	Himalayas	India	23,184	7,066
Revolution Peak	Pamirs	Tajikistan	22,880	6,974

Aconcagua	Andes	Argentina	22,834	6,960
Ojos del Salado	Andes	Argentina/Chile	22,664	6,908
Bonete	Andes	Argentina/Chile	22,546	6,872
Ama Dablam	Himalayas	Nepal	22,494	6,856
Tupungato	Andes	Argentina/Chile	22,310	6,800
Moscow Peak	Pamirs	Tajikistan	22,260	6,785
Pissis	Andes	Argentina	22,241	6,779
Mercedario	Andes	Argentina/Chile	22,211	6,770
Huascarán	Andes	Peru	22,205	6,768
Llullaillaco	Andes	Argentina/Chile	22,057	6,723
El Libertador	Andes	Argentina	22,047	6,720
Cachi	Andes	Argentina	22,047	6,720
Kailas	Himalayas	Tibet	22,027	6,714
Incahuasi	Andes	Argentina/Chile	21,720	6,620
Yerupaja	Andes	Peru	21,709	6,617
Kurumda	Pamirs	Tajikistan	21,686	6,610
Galan	Andes	Argentina	21,654	6,600
El Muerto	Andes	Argentina/Chile	21,463	6,542
Sajama	Andes	Bolivia	21,391	6,520
Nacimiento	Andes	Argentina	21,302	6,493
Illampu	Andes	Bolivia	21,276	6,485
Illimani	Andes	Bolivia	21,201	6,462
Laudo	Andes	Argentina	20,997	6,400
Ancohuma	Andes	Bolivia	20,958	6,388
Cuzco (Ausangate)	Andes	Peru	20,945	6,384
Tres Cruces	Andes	Argentina/Chile	20,853	6,356
Huandoy	Andes	Peru	20,852	6,356
Parinacota	Andes	Bolivia/Chile	20,768	6,330
Tortolas	Andes	Argentina/Chile	20,745	6,323
Chimborazo	Andes	Ecuador	20,702	6,310
Ampato	Andes	Peru	20,702	6,310
El Condor	Andes	Argentina	20,669	6,300
Salcantay	Andes	Peru	20,574	6,271
Huancarhuas	Andes	Peru	20,531	6,258

Famatina	Andes	Argentina	20,505	6,250
Solo	Andes	Argentina	20,492	6,246
Polleras	Andes	Argentina	20,456	6,235
Pular	Andes	Chile	20,423	6,225
Chañi	Andes	Argentina	20,341	6,200
McKinley (Denali)	Alaska	Alaska	20,320	6,194
Aucanquilcha	Andes	Chile	20,295	6,186
Juncal	Andes	Argentina/Chile	20,276	6,180
Negro	Andes	Argentina	20,184	6,152
Condoriri	Andes	Bolivia	20,095	6,125
Palermo	Andes	Argentina	20,079	6,120
Solimana	Andes	Peru	20,068	6,117
San Juan	Andes	Argentina/Chile	20,049	6,111
Sierra Nevada	Andes	Argentina	20,023	6,103
Marmolejo	Andes	Argentina/Chile	20,013	6,100

LARGEST DESERTS

Desert	Location	Size	Topography
Subtropical Deserts			
Sahara	Morocco, Western Sahara, Algeria, Tunisia, Libya, Egypt, Contrary to popular belief, the desert is only 30% sand. The world's largest nonpolar desertgets its name from the Arabic word Sahara', meaning desert Mauritania, Mali, Niger, Chad, Ethiopia, Eritrea, Somalia	3.5 million sq. mi.	70% gravel plains, sand, and dunes.

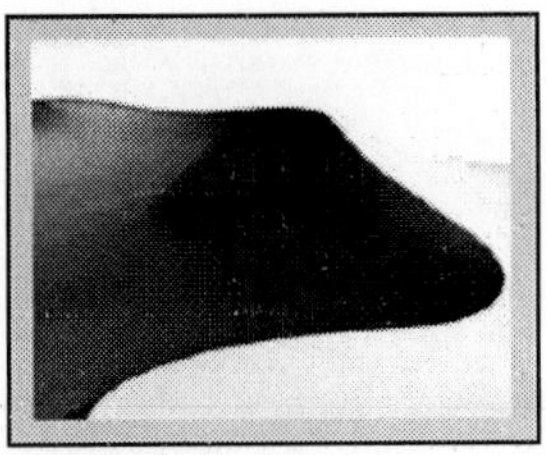

Arabian	Saudi Arabia, Kuwait, Qatar, United Arab Emirates, Oman, Yemen	1 million sq. mi.	Gravel plains, rocky highlands; one- fourth is the Rub al-Khali ("Empty Quarter"), the world's largest expanse of unbroken sand
Kalahari	Botswana, South Africa, Namibia	220,000 sq.mi.	Sand sheets, longitudinal dunes
Australian Desert Gibson	Australia (southern portion of the Western Desert)	120,000 sq.mi.	Sandhills, gravel, grass. These three regions of desert
Great Sandy	Australia (northern portion are of the Western Desert)	150,000 sq.mi.	collectively are of referred to as the Desert—otherwise
Great Victoria	Australia (southern most portion of the Western Desert)	250,000sq.mi.	known as "the Outback." Contains Ayers Rock, or Uluru, one of the world's largest monoliths
Simpson & Sturt Stony	Australia (eastern half of the continent)	56,000 sq. mi.	Simpson's straight, parallel sand dunes are the longest in the world—up to 125 mi. Encompasses the Stewart Stony Desert, named for the Australian explorer
Mojave	U.S.: Arizona, Colorado, Nevada, Utah, California	54,000 sq. mi.	Mountain chains, dry alkaline lake beds, calcium carbonatedunes
Sonoran	U.S.: Arizona, California; Mexico	120,000 sq.mi.	Basins and plains bordered by mountain ridges; home to the Saguarocactus
Chihuahuan	Mexico; southwestern U.S.	175,000 sq.mi.	Shrub desert; largestin North America
Thar	India, Pakistan	175,000 sq.mi.	Rocky sand and sand dunes

COOL COASTAL DESERTS

Namib	Angola, Namibia, South Africa	13,000 sq. mi.	Gravel plains
Atacama	Chile	54,000 sq. mi.	Salt basins, sand, lava; world's driestdesert

COLD WINTER DESERTS

Great Basin	U.S.: Nevada, Oregon, Utah	190,000 sq.mi.	Mountain ridges, valleys, 1% sanddunes
Colorado Plateau	U.S.: Arizona, Colorado, New Mexico, Utah, Wyoming	130,000 sq.mi.	Sedimentary rock, mesas, andplateaus—includes the Grand Canyon and is also called the "Painted Desert" because of the spectacular colors inits rocks and canyons
Patagonian	Argentina	260,000 sq.mi.	Gravel plains, plateaus, basaltsheets
Kara-Kum	Uzbekistan, Turkmenistan	135,000 sq.mi.	90% gray layered sand — name means"black sand"
Kyzyl-Kum	Uzbekistan, Turkmenistan, Kazakhstan	115,000 sq.mi.	Sands, rock—name means "red sand"
Iranian	Iran	100,000 sq.mi.	Salt, gravel, rock
Taklamakan	China	105,000 sq.mi.	Sand, dunes, gravel
Gobi	China, Mongolia	500,000 sq.mi.	Stony, sandy soil, steppes (drygrasslands)

POLAR

Arctic	U.S., Canada, Greenland, Iceland, Norway, Sweden, Finland, Russia	5.4 million sq. mi.	Snow, glaciers, tundra
Antarctic	Antarctica	5.5 million sq.mi.	Ice, snow, bedrock

POLAR REGIONS

Antarctica

The second smallest continent, mostly south of the Antarctic Circle.

Area: 14.2 million sq. km (5.5 million sq. mi.).

Geographic South Pole: Earth's southernmost point, at latitude 90°S, where all lines of longitude meet.

Magnetic South Pole: The magnetic South Pole shifts about 5 miles (km) a year and is now located at about 66°S and 139°E on the Adélie Coast of Antarctica.

Terrain: About 98% thick ice sheet and 2% barren rock; glaciers form ice shelves along about half of the coastline, and floating ice shelves constitute 11% of the area of the continent.

Ice sheet: The continental ice sheet contains approximately 7 million cubic miles (30 million cu km) of ice, representing about 90% of the world's total.

Major ice shelves: Amery, Filchner, Larsen, Ronne, Ross. Ice shelves make up about 10% of Antarctica's ice, and are floating sheets of ice attached to land that project out into coastal waters.

Climate: The coldest, windiest, driest continent.

Regions: East Antarctica (c. 3,000,000 sq. mi./7,770,000 sq. km), the largest portion of the continent, is a high, ice-covered plateau. West Antarctica (c. 2,500,000 sq. mi./6,475,000 sq. km), is an archipelago of mountainous islands connected by ice. A mountain range divides them.

Elevation extremes

Lowest point: Bentley Subglacial Trench –8,327 ft. below sea level (–2,538 m)—the lowest land elevation is hidden within the trench. Highest point: Vinson Massif 16,066 ft. (4,897 m), Ellsworth Mountains.

The Arctic

Region, primarily made up of the frozen Arctic Ocean, that surrounds the North Pole. Land masses include islands and the northern parts of the European, Asian, and North American continents.

Area: 14.056 million sq. km (5.4 million sq. mi.), largely frozen ocean. Geographic North Pole: Northern end of Earth's axis, located at about latitude 90°N.

Magnetic North Pole: Continues to shift and is located at approximately 82°N and 114°W in the Queen Elizabeth Islands of northern Canada.

Terrain: Central surface covered by a perennial drifting polar icepack that averages about 3 meters in thickness; the icepack is surrounded by open seas during the summer, but more than doubles in size during the winter and extends to the encircling landmasses.

Climate: Polar climate characterized by persistent cold and relatively narrowannualtemperatureranges; winterscharacterizedbycontinuous darkness, cold and stable weather conditions, and clear skies; summers characterized by continuous daylight, damp and foggy weather, and weak cyclones with rain or snow.

Regions: The Arctic is divided by the summer isotherm, a climatic boundary between regions with summer temperatures averaging 50°F (or 10°C)—the subarctic—and colder regions (the true Arctic).

Elevation extremes: Lowest point: Fram Basin –4,665 m. Highest point: sea level 0 m.

DEADLIEST VOLCANIC ERUPTIONS

Volcano	Year	Deaths	Major cause of deaths
Tambora, Indonesia	1815	92,000	Starvation
Krakatau, Indonesia	1883	36,417	Tsunami
Mount Pelee, Martinique	1902	29,025	Ash flows
Ruiz, Colombia	1985	25,000	Mudflows
Unzen, Japan	1792	14,300	Volcano collapse, tsunami
Laki, Iceland	1783	9,350	Starvation
Kelut, Indonesia	1919	5,110	Mudflows
Galunggung, Indonesia	1882	4,011	Mudflows
Vesuvius, Italy	1631	3,500	Mudflows, lava flows
Vesuvius, Italy	79	3,360	Ash flows, falls
Papandayan, Indonesia	1772	2,957	Ash flows
Lamington, Papua New Guinea	1951	2,942	Ash flows
El Chichon, Mexico	1982	2,000	Ash flows
Soufriere, St. Vincent	1902	1,680	Ash flows
Oshima, Japan	1741	1,475	Tsunami
Asama, Japan	1783	1,377	Ash flows, mudflows
Taal, Philippines	1911	1,335	Ash flows
Mayon, Philippines	1814	1,200	Mudflows

Agung, Indonesia	1963	1,184	Ash flows
Cotopaxi, Ecuador	1877	1,000	Mudflows
Pinatubo, Philippines	1991	800	Disease
Komagatake, Japan	1640	700	Tsunami
Ruiz, Colombia	1845	700	Mudflows
Hibok-Hibok, Philippines	1951	500	Ash flows

RECENT VOLCANIC ACTIVITY

Volcano	Year of last eruption or activity
Akan, Hokkaido, Japan	2006
Ambrym Island, Vanuatu	2007
Amukta, Alaska	1996
Anatahan, Mariana Islands	2007
Aoba, Ambae Island, Vanuatu	2006
Arenal, Costa Rica	ongoing
Aso, Kyushu, Japan	2004
Atka, Aleutian Islands, United States	2006
Augustine, Cook Inlet, Alaska, United States	2006
Bamus, New Britain Island, Papua New Guinea	2006
Bandai, Honshu, Japan	2000
Barren Island, Indian Ocean	2007
Batu Tara, Lesser Sunda Islands, Indonesia	2007
Bezymianny, Kamchatka, Russia	2007
Bromo, Java, Indonesia	2000
Bulusan, Philippines	2007
Mount Cameroon, Cameroon	2000
Canlaon, Philippines	2006
Chaitén, Chile	2008
Chikurachki, Kurile Islands, Russia	2005
Chiginagak, Alaska	1997
Chuginadak, Alaska	2005
Cleveland, Chuginadak Island, Alaska	2006
Conception, Island of Ometepe, Nicaragua	2007
Copahue, Argentina and Chile	2000
Dempo, Sumatra Indonesia	2006

East Epi, Vanuatu	2004
Ebeko, Kuril Islands, Russia	2007
Egoni, Indonesia	2004
Erta Ale, Ethiopia	2003
Etna, Sicily, Italy	2007
Fourpeaked, Alaska Peninsula, United States	2006
Fukutoku-Okanoba, Japan	2005
Galeras, Colombia	2007
Gamalama, Indonesia	2003
Grimsvotn, Iceland	1998
Guagua Pichincha, Ecuador	2006
Hachijo-Jima, Izu Islands, Japan	2002
Hakkoda, Japan	1997
Heard Island, Southern Indian Ocean, Australia	2006
Hekla, Iceland	2000
Mount Hili Aludo, Indonesia	1997
Hokkaido, Japan	2006
Home Reef, Tonga Islands, Tonga	2006
Hosho, Kyushu, Japan	1995
Ijen, Java, Indonesia	2001
Iwate-san, Honshu, Japan	1998
Jackson Segment, N. Gorda Ridge (nr. Oregon)	2001
Kaba, Sumatra, Indonesia	2000
Mount Karangetang, Indonesia	2007
Karthala, Comoros Islands, Indian Ocean	2007
Kavachi Seamount, Solomon Islands	2004
Kelut, Java, Indonesia	2006
Kick-'em-Jenny (nr. Grenada)	2003
Kikai, Japan	2004
Kliuchevskoi, Kamchatka, Russia	2007
Komagatake, Hokkaido, Japan	2000
Korovin, Alaska	1998
Krakatau, Indonesia	2001
Langila, New Britain, P.N.G.	2007
Lamongan, Indonesia	2003
Lascar, Chile	2007

Leroboleng, Indonesia	2003
Mount Lewotobi, Indonesia	2003
Llaima, Chile	2008
Lokon, Sulawesi, Indonesia	2003
Lopevi, Central Islands, Vanuatu	2007
La Madera, Nicaragua	1996
Maroa, New Zealand	2001
Mauna Loa, Hawaii	2003
Mayon, Philippines	2006
McDonald Island, Australia	1996
Merapi, Indonesia	2007
Metis Shoal, Tonga	1995
Momotombo, Nicaragua	1996
Monowai Seamount, Kermadec Islands	1997
Nevado Del Huila, Colombia	2007
Nyamuragira, Congo (Dem. Rep.)	2006
Nyiragongo, Congo (Dem. Rep.)	2003
Okmok, Alaska	1997
Ol Doinya Lengai, Tanzania, Africa	2006
Oyama, Miyake-jima, Izu Islands, Japan	2006
Pacaya, Guatemala	2007
Pagan, Mariana Islands, central Pacific Ocean	2006
Pago, Papua New Guinea	2004
Papandayan, Java, Indonesia	2002
Peuet Sague, Indonesia	1998
Piparo, Trinidad	1997
Piton de la Fournaise, Réunion	2007
Poas, Costa Rica	2006
Popocatepetl, Mexico	2007
Rabaul, Papua New Guinea	2007
Raoul Island, New Zealand	2006
Reventador, Ecuador	2007
Ritter Island, Papua New Guinea	2006
Rotorua, New Zealand	2001
Ruapehu, New Zealand	2006

San Cristobal, Nicaragua	2006
San Miguel, El Salvador	2006
Santa Ana, El Salvador	2006
Sendai, Japan	2011
Shiveluch, Kamchatka, Russia	ongoing
Shishaldin, Unimak Island, Alaska	2000
Simbo, Solomon Islands	2006
Slamet, Java Indonesia	2007
Soputan, Indonesia	2006
South Sister, Oregon	2001
Sulu Range, New Britain Island, Papua New Guinea	2006
Tavurvur, Papua New Guinea	2000
Taal, Philippines	2006
Talang, Indonesia	2007
Telica, Nicaragua	2007
Tengger Caldera, Java, Indonesia	2006
Terceira, Azores	1999
Tonga (unnamed volcano)	1999
Tongariro Volcanic Centre, New Zealand	2006
Turrialba, Costa Rica	2006
Ubinas, Peru	2007
Ulawun, Papua New Guinea	2007
Usu, Japan	2000
Veniaminof, Alaska	2006
Villarrica, Chile	2005
White Island, New Zealand	2007
Yasur, Tanna Island, Vanuatu	2004
Yellowstone, Wyoming	1998
Zacatecas, Mexico	1997

EARTHQUAKES

An earthquake is the result of a sudden release of stored energy in the Earth's crust that creates seismic waves. It is caused by tectonic plates getting stuck and putting a strain on the ground. The strain becomes so great that rocks give way by fault planes breaking. Smaller earthquakes can also be caused by volcanic activity.

Deadliest Earthquakes on Record (50,000 deaths or more)

Date	Location	Deaths	Magnitude
Jan. 23, 1556	Shansi, China	830,000	~8
July 27, 1976	Tangshan, China	255,0001	7.5
Aug. 9, 1138	Aleppo, Syria	230,000	n.a.
Dec. 26, 2004	Off west coast of northernSumatra	225,000+	9.0
Dec. 22, 8562	Damghan, Iran	200,000	n.a.
May 22, 1927	near Xining, Tsinghai, China	200,000	7.9
Dec. 16, 1920	Gansu, China	200,000	7.8
March 23, 8932	Ardabil, Iran	150,000	n.a.
Sept. 1, 1923	Kwanto, Japan	143,000	7.9
Oct. 5, 1948	Ashgabat, Turkmenistan,USSR	110,000	7.3
Dec. 28, 1908	Messina, Italy	70,000–100,0003	7.2
Sept. 1290	Chihli, China	100,000	n.a.
May 12, 2008	Eastern Sichuan, China	87,587	7.9
Oct. 8, 2005	Pakistan	80,361	7.6
Nov. 1667	Shemakha, Caucasia	80,000	n.a.
Nov. 18, 1727	Tabriz, Iran	77,000	n.a.
Dec. 25, 1932	Gansu, China	70,000	7.6
Nov. 1, 1755	Lisbon, Portugal	70,000	8.7
May 31, 1970	Peru	66,000	7.9
May 30, 1935	Quetta, Pakistan	30,000–60,000	7.5
Jan. 11, 1693	Sicily, Italy	60,000	n.a.
1268	Silicia, Asia Minor	60,000	n.a.
June 20, 1990	Iran	50,000	7.7
Feb. 4, 1783	Calabria, Italy	50,000	n.a.
March 11, 2011	Sendai, Japan	20,000	9.0
August 11, 2012	East Azerbaijan Province,Iran	360	9.9
Sept. 24, 2013	Balochistan, Pakistan	825	7.7
August 3, 2014	Ludian County, China	729	10.0
April 25, 2015	Nepal	8964	7.8
Sept. 8, 2017	Mexico	370	8.2
August 14, 2021	Haiti	2,200	7.2
February 6, 2023	Turkey & Syria	59,000	7.8 & 7.5
March 28, 2025	Myanmar	5380	7.7

WORLD'S LARGEST DAMS

Dam	Location	Volume (thousands) Cu m	Cuyds	Year
Three Gorges	China	39,300,000	51,402,459	UC08
Syncrude Tailings	Canada	540,000	706,320	UC
Chapetón	Argentina	296,200	387,410	UC
Pati	Argentina	238,180	274,026	UC
New Cornelia Tailings	United States	209,500	274,026	1973
Tarbela	Pakistan	121,720	159,210	1976
Kambaratinsk	Kyrgyzstan	112,200	146,758	UC
Fort Peck	Montana	96,049	125,628	1940
Lower Usuma	Nigeria	93,000	121,644	1990
Cipasang	Indonesia	90,000	117,720	UC
Atatürk	Turkey	84,500	110,522	1990
Yacyretá-Apipe	Paraguay/ Argentina	81,000	105,944	1998
Guri (Raúl Leoni)	Venezuela	78,000	102,014	1986
Rogun	Tajikistan	75,500	98,750	1985
Oahe	South Dakota	70,339	92,000	1963
Mangla	Pakistan	65,651	85,872	1967
Gardiner	Canada	65,440	85,592	1968
Afsluitdijk	Netherlands	63,400	82,927	1932
Oroville	California	59,639	78,008	1968
San Luis	California	59,405	77,700	1967
Nurek	Tajikistan	58,000	75,861	1980
Garrison	North Dakota	50,843	66,500	1956
Cochiti	New Mexico	48,052	62,850	1975
Tabka (Thawra)	Syria	46,000	60,168	1976
Bennett W.A.C.	Canada	43,733	57,201	1967
Tucuruíi	Brazil	43,000	56,242	1984
Boruca	Costa Rica	43,000	56,242	UC
High Aswan (Sadd-el- Aali)	Egypt	43,000	56,242	1970
San Roque	Philippines	43,000	56,242	UC
Kiev	Ukraine	42,841	56,034	1964

Dantiwada Left Embankment	India	41,040	53,680	1965
Saratov	Russia	40,400	52,843	1967
Mission Tailings	Arizona	40,088	52,435	1973
Fort Randall	South Dakota	38,227	50,000	1953
Kanev	Ukraine	37,860	49,520	1976
Mosul	Iraq	36,000	47,086	1982
Kakhovka	Ukraine	35,640	46,617	1955
Itumbiara	Brazil	35,600	46,563	1980
Lauwerszee	Netherlands	35,575	46,532	1969
Beas	India	35,418	46,325	1974
Oosterschelde	Netherlands	35,000	45,778	1986

STOCK EXCHANGES AROUND THE WORLD

A stock exchange, share market or bourse is a corporation or mutual organization which provides facilities for stock brokers and traders, to trade company stocks and other securities. Stock exchanges also provide facilities for the issue and redemption of securities, as well as, other financial instruments and capital events including the payment of income and dividends.

List of Stock Exchanges

- In South Africa: JSE Securities Exchange / Johannesburg Stock Exchange (JSE), The South Mrican Futures Exchange (SAFEX), Alternative Exchange (ALTX), Bond Exchange of South Mrica (BESA)
- In Australia: Australia Pacific Exchange (APX), Australian Stock Exchange (ASX), Bendigo Stock Exchange (BSX), National Stock Exchange of Australia (NSX) formerly Newcastle Stock Exchange, Sydney Futures Exchange (SFE)
- In India: Ahmedabad Stock Exchange, Bangalore Stock Exchange, Bhubaneswar Stock Exchange (BhSE), Bombay (Mumbai) Stock Exchange (BSE), Calcutta (kolkata) Stock Exchange, Cochin Stock Exchange, Coimbatore Stock Exchange, Delhi Stock Exchange Association, Guwahati Stock Exchange, Hyderabad Stock Exchange, Inter-connected Stock Exchange of India, Jaipur Stock Exchange, Ludhiana Stock Exchange Association, Madhya Pradesh Stock

Exchange, Madras Stock Exchange, Mangalore Stock Exchange, National Stock Exchange of India (NSE), OTC Exchange of India, Pune Stock Exchange, Saurashtra-Kutch Stock Exchange, Uttar Pradesh Stock Association, Vadodara Stock Exchange

- In Japan: Fukuoka Stock Exchange,Hiroshima Stock Exchange(Merger with Tokyo Stock Exchange), JASDAQ, Kobe Stock Exchange (Closed in 1967), Kyoto Stock Exchange (Merger with Osaka Securities Exchange), Nagoya Stock Exchange (NSE), Niigata Stock Exchange(Merger with Tokyo Stock Exchange), Nippon New Market Hercules.
- In Malaysia: Kuala Lumpur Stock Exchange (Bursa Malaysia) (KLSE), Kuala Lumpur Commodity Exchange, Kuala Lumpur Options and Financial Futures Exchange, MESDAQ
- In Pakistan: Islamabad Stock Exchange (ISE), Karachi Stock Exchange (KSE), Lahore Stock Exchange (LSE)
- In Singapore: Stock Exchange of Singapore (SES), precursor to Singapore Exchange, Singapore Exchange (SGX)
- In Germany: Berliner Borse, Borse Hamburg, Borse Hannover, Borse Miinchen, Borse Stuttgart, Borse Dusseldorf, Frankfurt Stock Exchange (owned by Deutsche Borse; Index: DAX)
- In Poland: Warsaw Stock Exchange (WSE, GPW - Gie3da Papier6w Wartoreciowych Warszawie)
- In Russia: Moscow Interbank Currency Exchange (MICEX), RTS Stock Exchange, Saint Petersburg Stock Exchange (SPBEX)
- In United Kingdom: London Stock Exchange (FTSE 100 Index)
- In North America: see List of American stock exchanges for more information.
- In Mexico: Bolsa Mexicana de Valores (BMV)
- In United States of America: Archipelago Exchange, merged with NYSE, Ariwna Stock Exchange, closed down, American Stock Exchange (AMEX), Boston Stock Exchange, Chicago Stock Exchange, HedgeStreet
- In Central America: See List of American stock exchanges for more information.

- In South America: See List of American stock exchanges for more information.
- In Brazil: Bovespa (State of Sao Paulo Stock Exchange), Rio de Janeiro Stock Exchange (BVRJ), Brazilian Mercantile and Futures Exchange (BM and F), Maringa Mercantile and Futures Exchange.

Top Three Stock Exchanges

- New York Stock Exchange (NYSE) - the largest stock exchange in the world by dollar volume and over 2500 listed securities. NYSE is operated by NYSE Euronext, the holding company created by the combination of NYSE Group, Inc. and Euronext N.V. NYSE is a world leader for listings, trading in cash equities, equity and interest rate derivatives, bonds and the distribution of market data.
- Tokyo Stock Exchange - the second largest stock exchange market in the world by market value. Lists 2,271 domestic companies and 31 foreign companies, with a total market capitalization of over 5 trillion USD.
- London Stock Exchange - the world's oldest stock exchange and one of the top three stock exchanges in the world. Lists around 3000 companies. Total equity turnover value of more than 3.5 billion.

THE SEVEN WONDERS OF THE ANCIENT WORLD

- The Great Pyramid of Giza
- The Hanging Gardens of Babylon
- The Temple of Artemis at Ephesus
- The Statue of Zeus at Olympia
- The Mausoleum at Halicarnassus
- The Colossus of Rhodes
- The Pharos of Alexandria

THE EIGHT WONDERS OF THE MODERN WORLD

- The Empire State Building
- The Itaipú Dam

- The Panama Canal
- The Channel Tunnel
- The North Sea Protection Works
- The Golden Gate Bridge
- The Taj Mahal
- Angkor Wat, Cambodia

Awards and Honours

6

NOBEL PRIZE AWARD

The Nobel Prizes are awards in Physics, Chemistry, Literature, Peace, Physiology or Medicine and Economics.

The Nobel Prize Winners - 2024

Physics	:	Pierre Agostini, Ferenc Krausz, Anne L'Huillier
Chemistry	:	Moungi Bawendi, Louis Brus, Aleksey Yekimov
Medicine	:	Katalin Karikó, Drew Weissman
Literature	:	Jon Fosse
Peace	:	Narges Mohammadi
Economics	:	Claudia Goldin

The Nobel Prize Winners - 2023

Physics	:	John J. Hopfield, Geoffrey Hinton
Chemistry	:	David Baker; Demis Hassabis & John Jumper
Medicine	:	Victor Ambros, Gary Ruvkun
Literature	:	Han Kang
Peace	:	Nihon Hidankyo
Economics	:	Daron Acemoglu, Simon Johnson, James A. Robinson

IEEE JOHN VON NEUMANN MEDAL

The IEEE John von Neumann Medal was established by the IEEE Board of Directors in 1990 and may be presented annually "for outstanding achievements in computer-related science and technology." The achievements may be theoretical, technological, or entrepreneurial, and need not have been made immediately prior to the date of the award.

2000: John L. Hennessy and David A. Patterson
2001: Butler W. Lampson
2002: Ole-Johan Dahl and Kristen Nygaard
2003: Alfred V. Aho
2004: Barbara H. Liskov
2005: Michael Stonebraker
2006: Edwin Catmull
2007: Charles P. Thacker 2
2008: Leslie Lamport
2009: Susan L. Graham
2010: John Hopcroft and Jeffrey Ullman
2011: C.A.R. (TONY) Hoare
2012: Edward McCluskey
2013: Jack B. Dennis
2014: Cleve Moler
2015: James A. Gosling
2016: Christos Harilaos Papadimitriou
2017: Valamidir Vapnik
2018 : Patrick Cousot
2019: Eva Tardos
2020: Michael I.Jordan
2021: Jeffery Dean
2022: Deborah Estrini
2023: Tom Leighton
2024: Christopher D.Manning
2025: Miklos Ajtai

THE MAN BOOKER PRIZE

The Man Booker Prize for Fiction, also known as the Booker Prize, is one of the world's most prestigious literary prizes, awarded each year for the best original full-length novel, written in English by a citizen of the Commonwealth of Nations or the Republic of Ireland.

Year	Person	Book	Nationality
2000	Margaret Atwood	The Blind Assassin	Canada
2001	Peter Carey	True History of the Kelly Gang	Australia
2002	Yann Martel	Life of Pi	Canada
2003	DBC Pierre	Vernon God Little	Australia
2004	Alan Hollinghurst	The Line of Beauty	United Kingdom
2005	John Banville	The Sea	Ireland
2006	Kiran Desai	The Inheritance of Loss	India
2007	Anne Enright	The Gathering	Ireland
2008	Aravind Adiga	The White Tiger	India
2009	Hilary Mantel	Wolf Hall	United Kingdom
2010	Howard Jacobson	The Finkler Question	United
2011	Julian Barnes	The Sense of an Ending	United Kingdom
2012	Hilary Mantel	Bring Up the Bodies	United Kingdom
2013	Eleanor Catton	The Luminaries	New Zealand
2014	Richard Flanagan	The Narrow Road to the Deep North	Australia
2015	Marlon James	A Brief History of Seven Killings	Jamaica
2016	Paul Beatty	The Sellout	United States
2017	George Saunders	Lincoln in the Bardo	United States
2018	Anna Burns	Milkman	United Kingdom
2019	Margaret Atwood & Bernardine Evaristo	The Testaments & Girl, Woman, Other	Canada / United Kingdom
2020	Douglas Stuart	Shuggie Bain	United States
2021	Damon Galgut	The Promise	South Africa
2022	Shehan Karunatilaka	The Seven Moons of Maali Almeida	Sri Lanka
2024	Samantha Harvey	Orbital	Britain
2025	David Szalay	Flesh	Hungarian-British

ALBERT EINSTEIN WORLD AWARD FOR SCIENCE

The Albert Einstein World Award for Science is a yearly award given by the World Cultural Council as a means of recognition, and as an incentive to scientific and technological research and development. The award has been named after Albert Einstein and includes a diploma, a commemorative medal, and $10,000.

Eske Willetslev

List of Winners

2024 : Eske Willetslev

2023 : ChristophGerber

2022: Victoria M. Kaspi
2019 : Zhonghin Wang
2018 : Jean--Pierre Changeux
2017 : Omar M.Yaghi
2016 : Edward Witten
2015 : Ewine van Dishoeck
2014 : Philip Cohen
2013 : Paul Nurse
2012 : Michael Grätzel
2011 : Geoffrey Alan Ozin
2010 : Julio Montaner

Edward Witten

GRAMMY AWARDS

The Grammy Awards (originally called the Gramophone Awards) are presented annually by the National Academy of Recording Arts and Sciences of the United States for outstanding achievements in the record industry.

Year	Record of the year	Song of the year	Album of the year	Best new artist
2010	"Need You Now," Lady Antebellum	"Need You Now," Lady Antebellum	The Suburbs, Arcade Fire	Esperanza Spalding
2011	"Rolling in the Deep," Adele	"Rolling in the Deep," Adele	21, Adele	Bon Iver
2012	"Somebody That I Used to Know," Gotye featuring Kimbra	"We Are Young," Fun. featuring Janelle Monáe	Babel, Mumford & Sons	Fun.
2013	"Get Lucky," Daft Punk featuring Pharrell Williams and Nile Rodgers	"Royals," Lorde	Random Access Memories, Daft Punk	Macklemore & Ryan Lewis
2014	"Stay with Me," Sam Smith	"Stay with Me," Sam Smith	Morning Phase, Beck	Sam Smith
2015	"Uptown Funk," Mark Ronson featuring Bruno Mars	"Thinking Out Loud," Ed Sheeran and Amy Wadge	1989, Taylor Swift	Meghan Trainor

2016	"Hello," Adele	"Hello," Adele and Greg Kurstin	25, Adele	Chance the Rapper
2017	"24K Magic," Bruno Mars	"That's What I Like," Bruno Mars	24K Magic, Bruno Mars	Alessia Cara
2018	"This Is America," Childish Gambino	"This Is America," Childish Gambino	Golden Hour, Kacey Musgraves	Dua Lipa
2019	"Bad Guy," Billie Eilish	"Bad Guy," Billie Eilish	When We All Fall Asleep, Where Do We Go?, Billie Eilish	Billie Eilish
2020	"Everything I Wanted,"Billie Eilish	"I Can't Breathe," H.E.R.	Folklore, Taylor Swift	Megan Thee Stallion
2021	"Leave the Door Open," Silk Sonic	"Leave the Door Open," Silk Sonic	We Are, Jon Batiste	Olivia Rodrigo
2022	"About Damn Time," Lizzo	"Just Like That," Bonnie Raitt	Harry's House, Harry Styles	Samara Joy
2023	"Flowers," Miley Cyrus	"What Was I Made For," Billie Eilish	Midnights, Taylor Swift	Victoria Monét
2024	"Not Like Us," Kendrick Lamar	"Not Like Us," Kendrick Lamar	Cowboy Carter, Beyoncé	Chappell Roan

MISS UNIVERSE

Haarnaaz Sandhu

Miss Universe is an annual international beauty contest. The title for the winner of the contest was founded in 1952 by California clothing company Pacific Mills. The pageant is currently run by the Miss Universe Organization.

2005	Canada	Natalie Glebova	23	5′11"	Miss Universe Canada
2006	Puerto Rico	Zuleyka Rivera	18	5′9"	Miss Puerto Rico Universe
2007	Japan	Riyo Mori	21	5′9"	Miss Universe Japan
2008	Venezuela	Dayana Mendoza	22	5′9½″	Miss Venezuela
2009	Venezuela	Stefania Fernandez	18	5′10½″	Miss Venezuela
2010	Mexico	Ximena Navarrete	22	5′9"	Nuestra Belleza México
2011	Angola	Leila Lopes	25	5′10"	Benguela
2012	USA	Olivia Culpo	20	5′5"	Cranston

2013	Venezuela	Gabriela Isler	25	5′10"	Valencia
2014	Colombia	Paulina Vega	22	5′9"	Barranquilla
2015	Philippines	Pia Wurtzbach	26	5′8"	Cagayan de Oro
2016	France	Iris Mittenaere			
2017	South Africa	Deme Leigh Nel			
2018	Philippines	Coitriona Goray			
2019	South Africa	Zozibini Tunzi			
2020	Maxico	Andrea Meza			
2021	India	Haarnaaz Sandhu			
2022	America	R' Bonney Gabriel			
2023	Nicaragua	Sheynnis zpalacios			
2024	Denmark	Victoria Kajaer			

MISS WORLD

Suchata Chuangsri

The Miss World pageant is an international beauty pageant, founded in the United Kingdom by Eric Morley in 1951.

2014	South Africa	Rolene Strauss	April 22, 1992	London, UK	ExCeL London
2015	Spain	Mireia Lalaguna	November 28, 1992	Sanya, China	Crown of Beauty Theatre
2016	USA	Puerto Rico			
2017	India	Manushi Chillar			
2018	Mexico	Vanessa Ponce			
2019	Jamaica	Toni Ann Singh			
2020	No Competition held due to Kovid				
2021	Poland	Karolina Bielawska			
2022	No Cometition held due to delay.				
2023	Czech Republic	Krystyna Pyszkova			
2024	No competition held due to delay competition in 2023.				
2025	Thailand	Suchata Chuangsri			

❑❑❑

Olympic Games

7

LIST OF 2024 SUMMER OLYMPICS MEDAL WINNERS

Athletics (Men)

Event	Gold	Silver	Bronze
100 metres	Noah Lyles. United States	Kishane Thompson, Jamaica	Fred Kerley United States
200 metres	Letsile Tebogo Botswana	Kenny Bednarek USA	Noah Lyles United States
400 metres	Quincy Hall USA	Matthew Hudson-Smith Great Britain	Muzala Samukonga Zambia
800 metres	Emmanuel Wanyonyi Kenya	Marco Arop Canada	Djamel Sedjati Algeria
1500 metres	Cole Hocker USA	Josh Kerr Great Britain	Yared Nuguse USA
5000 metres	Jakob Ingebrigtsen Norway	Ronald Kwemoi Kenya	Grant Fisher United States
10,000 metres	Joshua Cheptegei Uganda		Berihu Aregawi Ethiopia
Grant Fisher United States			
110 metres hurdles	Grant Holloway United States	Daniel Roberts United States	Rasheed Broadbell Jamaica
400 metres hurdles	Rai Benjamin United States	Karsten Warholm Norway	Alison dos Santos Brazil
3000 metres steeplechase	Soufiane El Bakkali Morocco	Kenneth Rooks United States	Abraham Kibiwot Kenya

Athletics (Women)

Event	Gold	Silver	Bronze
100 metres	Julien Alfred	Sha'Carri Richardson	Melissa Jefferson

	Saint Lucia	United States	United States
200 metres	Gabby Thomas United States	Julien Alfred Saint Lucia	Brittany Brown United States
400 metres	Marileidy Paulino Dominican Republic	Salwa Eid Naser Bahrain	Natalia Kaczmarek Poland
800 metres	Keely Hodgkinson Great Britain	Tsige Duguma Ethiopia	Mary Moraa Kenya
1500 metres	Faith Kipyegon Kenya	Jessica Hull Australia	Georgia Bell Great Britain
5000 metres	Beatrice Chebet Kenya	Faith Kipyegon Kenya	Sifan Hassan Netherlands
10,000 metres	Beatrice Chebet Kenya	Nadia Battocletti Italy	Sifan Hassan Netherlands
100 metres hurdles	Masai Russell United States	Cyréna Samba-Mayela France	Jasmine Camacho-Quinn Puerto Rico

Swimming (Men)

Event	Gold	Silver	Bronze
100 m freestyle	Pan Zhanle China	Kyle Chalmers Australia	David Popovici Romania
200 m freestyle	David Popovici Romania	Matthew Richards Great Britain	Luke Hobson United States
400 m freestyle	Lukas Märtens Germany	Elijah Winnington Australia	Kim Woo-min South Korea
800 m freestyle	Daniel Wiffen Ireland	Bobby Finke USA	Gregorio Paltrinieri Italy
1500 m freestyle	Bobby Finke USA	Gregorio Paltrinieri Italy	Daniel Wiffen Ireland
100 m backstroke	Thomas Ceccon Italy	Xu Jiayu China	Ryan Murphy United States
200 m backstroke	Hubert Kós Hungary	Apostolos Christou Greece	Roman Mityukov Switzerland
100 m breaststroke	Nicolò Martinenghi Italy	Adam Peaty Great Britain Nic Fink United States	Not awarded as there was a tie for silver.
200 m breaststroke	Léon Marchand France	Zac Stubblety-Cook Australia	Caspar Corbeau Netherlands

Swimming (Women)

Event	Gold	Silver	Bronze
100 m freestyle	Sarah Sjöström Sweden	Torri Huske United States	Siobhán Haughey Hong Kong
200 m freestyle	Mollie O'Callaghan Australia	Ariarne Titmus Australia	Siobhán Haughey Hong Kong
400 m freestyle	Ariarne Titmus Australia	Summer McIntosh Canada	Katie Ledecky USA
800 m freestyle	Katie Ledecky USA	Ariarne Titmus Australia	Paige Madden USA

1500 m freestyle	Katie Ledecky USA	Anastasiya Kirpichnikova France	Isabel Marie Gose Germany
100 m backstroke	Kaylee McKeown Australia	Regan Smith United States	Katharine Berkoff United States
200 m backstroke	Kaylee McKeown Australia	Regan Smith USA	Kylie Masse Canada

Water Polo

Event	Gold	Silver	Bronze
Men	Serbia (SRB)	Croatia (CRO)	United States (USA)
Women	Spain	Australia	Netherlands

Badminton

Event	Gold	Silver	Bronze
Men's singles	Viktor Axelsen Denmark	Kunlavut Vitidsarn Thailand	Lee Zii Jia Malaysia
Men's doubles	Chinese Taipei Lee Yang Wang Chi-lin	China Liang Weikeng Wang Chang	Malaysia Aaron Chia Soh Wooi Yik
Women's singles	An Se-young South Korea	He Bingjiao China	Gregoria Mariska Tunjung Indonesia
Women's doubles	China Chen Qingchen Jia Yifan	China Liu Shengshu Tan Ning	Japan Nami Matsuyama Chiharu Shida

Basketball

Event	Gold	Silver	Bronze
Men	United States (USA)	France	Serbia (SRB)
Women	United States (USA)	France	Australia

Boxing Men's Events

Event	Gold	Silver	Bronze
Flyweight (51 kg)	Hasanboy Dusmatov Uzbekistan	Billal Bennama France	Junior Alcántara Dominican Republic Daniel Varela de Pina Cape Verde
Featherweight (57 kg)	Abdumalik Khalokov Uzbekistan	Munarbek Seiitbek Uulu Kyrgyzstan	Charlie Senior Australia Javier Ibáñez Bulgaria

Lightweight (63.5) kg	Erislandy Álvarez Cuba	Sofiane Oumiha France	Wyatt Sanford Canada Lasha Guruli Georgia

Boxing Women's Events

Event	Gold	Silver	Bronze
Flyweight (50 kg)	Wu Yu China	Buse Naz Çakiroglu Turkey	Nazym Kyzaibay Kazakhstan Aira Villegas Philippines
Bantamweight (54 kg)	Chang Yuan China	Hatice Akbas Turkey	Pang Chol-mi North Korea Im Ae-ji South Korea
Featherweight (57 kg)	Lin Yu-ting Chinese Taipei	Julia Szeremeta Poland	Esra Yildiz Turkey Nesthy Petecio Philippines

Hockey

Event	Gold	Silver	Bronze
Men	Netherlands	Germany	India
Women	Netherlands	China	Argentina

Football

Event	Gold	Silver	Bronze
Men	Spain	France	Morocco
Women	United States	Brazil	Germany

Handball

Event	Gold	Silver	Bronze
Men	Denmark (DEN)	Germany (GER)	Spain
Women	Norway (NOR)	France (FRA)	Denmark (DEN)

Wrestling Men's Freestyle

Event	Gold	Silver	Bronze
65 kg	Kotaro Kiyooka Japan	Rahman Amouzad Iran	Sebastian Rivera Puerto Rico Islam Dudaev Albania
74 kg	Razambek Zhamalov	Daichi Takatani Japan	Kyle Dake United States

	Uzbekistan		Chermen Valiev Albania
97 kg	Akhmed Tazhudinov Bahrain	Givi Matcharashvili Georgia	Magomedkhan Magomedov Azerbaijan Amir Ali Azarpira Iran
125 kg	Geno Petriashvili Georgia	Amir Hossein Zare Iran	Taha Akgül Turkey
			Giorgi Meshvildishvili Azerbaijan

Women's Freestyle

Event	Gold	Silver	Bronze
50 kg	Sarah Hildebrandt USA	Yusneylys Guzmán Cuba	Yui Susaki Japan Feng Ziqi China
53 kg	Akari Fujinami Japan	Lucía Yépez Ecuador	Choe Hyo-gyong North Korea Pang Qianyu China
57 kg	Tsugumi Sakurai Japan	Anastasia Nichita Moldova	Helen Maroulis United States Hong Kexin China
62 kg	Sakura Motoki Japan	Iryna Koliadenko Ukraine	Aisuluu Tynybekova Kyrgyzstan Grace Bullen Norway
68 kg	Amit Elor United States	Meerim Zhumanazarova Kyrgyzstan	Buse Tosun Çavusoglu Turkey Nonoka Ozaki Japan
76 kg	Yuka Kagami Japan	Kennedy Blades USA	Milaimys Marín Cuba Tatiana Rentería Colombia

❑❑❑

World Literature

8

MOST IMPORTANT BOOKS IN THE WORLD OF LITERATURE

Book Name	Author	Year
House Made of Dawn	N. Scott Momaday, United States	1972
Invisible Cities	Italo Calvino, Italy	1974
The Conservationist	Nadine Gordimer, South Mrica	1978
Red Sorghum	Mo Yan, China	1987
Rabindranath Tagore A Centenary Valume	J. M.S. Rawat	1992
Struggle for Freedom	Sisir Kumar Das	1995
The Story of Writting India's Crapt people	Nta Berry	1998
The Blind Assassin Canada	Margaret Atwood	2000
True History of the Kelly Gang Australia	Peter Carey	2001
Life of Pi Canada	Yann Martel	2002
Vernon God Little Australia	DBC Pierre	2003
The Line of Beauty United Kingdom	Alan Hollinghurst	2004
The Sea Ireland	John Banville	2005
The Inheritance of Loss India	Kiran Desai	2006
The Gathering Ireland	Anne Enright	2007
The White Tiger India	Aravind Adiga	2008
Wolf Hall United Kingdom	Hilary Mantel	2009
The Finkler Question United Kingdom	Howard Jacobson	2010
Visvakarma's Children Stones of	Jaya Jaitly	2011
Bring up the bodies	Hilary mantel	2012
Americanah	Chimamanda ngozi adichie	2013
All the light we cannot see	Anthony doerr	2014
10:04	Ben lerner	2015
The last of the soviets	Svetlana alexievich	2016

Lincoln in the Bardo	George Saunders	2017
Milkman	Anna Burns	2018
Normal People	Sally Rooney	2018
Girl, Woman, Other	Bernardine Evaristo	2019
The Testaments	Margaret Atwood	2019
Shuggie Bain	Douglas Stuart	2020
Klara and the Sun	Kazuo Ishiguro	2021
The Promise	Damon Galgut	2021
Demon Copperhead	Barbara Kingsolver	2022
The Seven Moons of Maali Almeida	Shehan Karunatilaka	2022
Time Shelter	Georgi Gospodinov	2023
Prophet Song	Paul Lynch	2023
The Bee Sting	Paul Murray	2023
Everything I Learned About Love	Dolly Alderton	2024
A Spell of Good Things	Ayobámi Adébáyo	2024
Cursed Bread	Sophie Mackintosh	2024
The Emperor of Gladness	Ocean Vuong	2025

FAMOUS BOOKS IN WORLD LITERATURE

The editors of the Norwegian Book Clubs, with the Norwegian Nobel Institute, polled a panel of 100 authors from 54 countries on what they considered the"best and most central works in world literature." Among the authors polled were Milan Kundera, Doris Lessing, Seamus Heaney, Salman Rushdie, Wole Soyinka, John Irving, Nadine Gordimer, and Carlos Fuentes. The list of 100 works appears alphabetically by author.

- Chinua Achebe, *Things Fall Apart*
- Hans Christian Andersen, *Fairy Tales and Stories*
- Jane Austen, *Pride and Prejudice*
- Honore de Balzac, *Old Father Goriot*
- Samuel Balzac, *Trilogy: Molloy, MaloneDies, The Unnamable*
- Giovanni Boccaccio, *Decameron*
- Jorge Luis Borges, *Collected Fictions*
- Emily Bronte, *Wuthering Heights*
- Albert Camus, *The Stranger*
- Paul Celan, *Poems*
- Louis-Ferdinand Celine, *Journey to the End of the Night*
- Miguel de Cervantes, *Don Quixote*

- Geoffrey Chaucer, *Canterbury Tales*
- Anton Chekhov, *Selected Stories; Thousand and One Nights*
- Joseph Conrad, *Nostromo*
- Dante Alighieri, *The Divine Comedy*
- Charles Dickens, *Great Expectations*
- Denis Diderot, *Jacques the Fatalist and His Master*
- Alfred Doblin, *Berlin Alexanderplatz*
- Fyodor Dostoyevsky, *Crime and Punishment; The Idiot; The Possessed; The Brothers Karamazov*
- George Eliot, *Middlemarch*
- Ralph Ellison, *Invisible Man*
- Euripides, *Medea*
- William Faulkner, *Absalom, Absalom; The Sound and the Fury*
- Gustave Flaubert, *Madame Bovary; A Sentimental Education*
- Federico Garcia Lorca, *Gypsy Ballads*
- Gabriel Garcia Marquez, *One Hundred Years of Solitude; Love in the Time of Cholera*
- Anon, *The Epic of Gilgamesh*
- Johann Wolfgang von Goethe, *Faust*
- Günter Grass, *The Tin Drum*
- Joao Guimaraes Rosa, *The Devil to Pay in the Backlands*
- Knut Hamsun, *Hunger*
- Ernest Hemingway, *The Old Man and the Sea*
- Homer, *The Iliad; The Odyssey*
- Anon, *The Book of Job*
- James Joyce, *Ulysses*
- Franz Kafka, *The Complete Stories; The Trial; The Castle*
- Kalidasa, *The Recognition of Sakuntala*
- Yasunari Kawabata, *The Sound of the Mountain*
- Nikos Kazantzakis, *Zorba the Greek*
- D. H. Lawrence, *Sons and Lovers*
- Giacomo Leopardi, *Complete Poems*
- Doris Lessing, *The Golden Notebook*
- Astrid Lindgren, *Pippi Longstocking*

- Lu Xun, *Diary of a Madman and Other Stories*
- Naguib Mahfouz, *Children of Gebelawi*
- Thomas Mann, *Buddenbrooks; The Magic Mountain*
- Michel de Montaigne, *Essays*
- Elsa Morante, *History*
- Toni Morrison, *Beloved*
- Murasaki Shikibu, *The Tale of Genji*
- Robert Musil, *The Man Without Qualities*
- George Orwell, *1984*
- Ovid, *Metamorphoses*
- Fernando Pessoa, *The Book of Disquiet*
- Edgar Allan Poe, *The Complete Tales*
- Marcel Proust, *Remembrance of Things Past*
- Juan Rulfo, *Pedro Paramo*
- Jalalu'l-Din Rumi, *The Mathnawi*
- Salman Rushdie, *Midnight's Children*
- Sheikh Saadi of Shiraz, *The Bostan of Saadi (The Orchard)*
- Jose Saramago, *Blindness*
- William Shakespeare, Hamlet; King Lear; *Othello*
- Sophocles, *Oedipus the King*
- Stendhal, *The Red and the Black*
- Laurence Sterne, *The Life and Opinions of Tristram Shandy*
- Jonathan Swift, *Gulliver's Travels*
- Leo Tolstoy, *War and Peace; Anna Karenina; The Death of Ivan Ilyich and Other Stories*
- Mark Twain, *The Adventures of Huckleberry Finn*
- Valmiki, *Ramayana*
- Walt Whitman, *Leaves of Grass*
- Virginia Woolf, *Mrs Dalloway; To the Lighthouse*
- Marguerite Yourcenar, *Memoirs of Hadrian*
- Arundhati Roy *The God of Small Things*

❑❑❑

Inventions and Discoveries

9

Adrenaline	(Isolation) John Jacob Abel, U.S., 1897.
Arosol can	Erik Rotheim, Norway, 1926
Air brake	George Westinghouse, U.S., 1868
Air conditioning	Will Carrier, U.S., 1911
Airship	(Non-rigid) Henri Giffard, France, 1852; (rigid) Ferdinand von Zepplin, Germany, 1900
Aluminium manufacture	(By electrolytic action) Charles M. Hall, U.S., 1866.)
Antiseptic	(Surgery) Joseph Lister, England, 1967.
Antitoxin, diphtheria	Emil von Behring, Germany, 1890.
Appliances, electric	(Fan) Schuyler Wheeler, U.S., 1882; (Flatiron) Henry W. Secly, U.S., 1882; (Stove) Hadaway, U.S., 1896; (Washing machine) Alva Fisher, U.S., 1906.
Aspirin	Dr. Felix Hoffman, Germany; 1899.
Astronomical calculator	The Antikythera device, first century B.C., Greece. Found off island of Antikythera in 1900.
Atom	(Nuclear model) Ernest Rutherford, England, 1911.
Atomic theory	(Ancient) Leucippus, Democritus, Greece, c. 500 RC.; Lucretius, Rome c.100 B.C.; olden) John Dalton, England, 1808.
Atomic structure	(Formulatednuclearmodelofatom,Rutherford model) Ernest Rutherford, England, 1911.
Automobile	(First with internal combustion engine, 250 rpm) Karl Benz, Germany; 1885; (First with practical high-speed internal Combustion engine, 900 rpm) Gottlieb Daimler, Germany; 1885; (First true

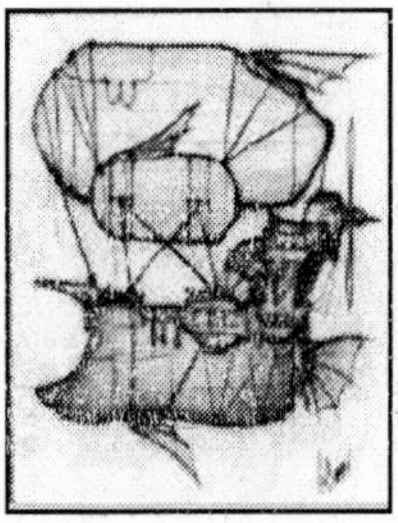

	automobile, not carriage with motor) Rene Panhard, Emile Lavassor, France, 1891; (Carburetor, spray) Charles E. Duryea, U.S., 1892.
Autopilot (For aircraft)	Ehner A. Sperry; U.S., c.1910, first successful test, 1912, in a Curtiss flying boat.
Avogadro's law	(Equal volumes of all gases at the same temperature and pressure contain equal number of molecules) Amedeo Avogadro, Italy, 1811.
Bacteria	Anton van Leeuwenhoek, The Netherlands, 1683.
Balloon (hotair)	Joseph and Jacques Montgolfier, France, 1783.
Barometer	Evangelista Torricelli, Italy; 1643.
Bicycle	Karl D. von Sauerbronn, Germany; 1816: (First modern model) James Starley; England, 1884.
Braille	Louis Braille, France, 1829.
Bullet (Conical)	Claude Minie, France, 1849.
Calculating machine	(Logarithms made multiplying easier and thus calculators practical) John Napier, Scotland, 1614.

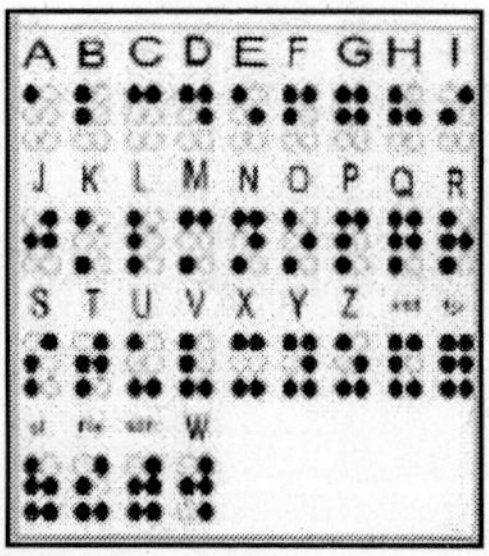

Calculus	Isaac Newton, England, 1669.
Camera	(Hand-held) George Eastman, U.S., 1888; (Polaroid Land) Edwin Land, U.S., 1948.
Carpet sweeper	Melville R. Bissell, U.S., 1876.
Car radio	William Lear, Elmer Wavering,U.S.,1929, manufactured by Galvin Manufacturing Co., 'Motorola.'
Chewing gum	(Spruce-based) John Curtis, U.S., 1848; (Chicle-blsed) Thomas Adams, U.S., 1870.
Clock (pendulum)	Christian Huygens, The Netherlands, 1656.
Coca-cola	John Pemberton, U.S.
Compact disk	RCA, U.S., 1972.
Computer	(First design of analytical engine) Charles Babbage, 1830s; (ENIAC, Electronic Numerical Integrator and Calculator, first all-electronic, completed) 1945;

	(Dedicated at Universiry of Pennsylvania) 1946; (UNIVAC, Universal Automatic Computer, handled both numeric and alphabetic data) 1951.
Condensed milk	Gail Borden, U.S., 1853.
Cosmetics	Egypt, c. 4000 B.C.
Cotton gin	Eli Whitney; U.S., 1793.
Dyn	(Aniline, start of synthetic dye industry) William H. Perkin, England, 1856.
Dynamite	Alfred Nobel, Sweden, 1867.
Electromagnet	William Sturgeon, England, 1823.
Election	Sir Joseph J. Thompson, England, 1897.
E = mc2	(Equivalence of mass and energy), Albert Einstein, Switzerland, 1907.
Expanding universe theory	(First proposed) George LeMaitre, Belgium, 1927; (Discovered first direct evidence that the universe is expanding Edwin P. Hubble, U.S., 1929; (Hubble constant a measure of the rate at which the universe is expanding) Edwin P. Hubble, U.S., 1929.
Falling bodies (law)	Galileo Galilei, Italy; 1590.
Fiber optics	Narinder Kapany; England, 1955.
Frozen food	Clarence Birdseye, U.S., 1924.
Gravitation (law)	Sir Isaac Newton, England, c. 1665 (published 1687).
Gunpowder	China, 700.
Halley's Comet	Edmund Halley, England, 1705.
Heart, implanted in human	Dr. Robert Jarvik:, U.S., 1982.
Helium first observed on sun	Sir Joseph Lockyer, England, 1868.

Holograph	Dennis Gabor, England, 1947.
Ice age theory	Louis Agassiz, Swiss-American, 1840.
Intelligence testing	Alfred Binet, Theodore Simon, France, 1905.
Laser	(Theoretical work on) Charles H.Townes, Arthur L. Schawlow, U.S., N. Basov, A. Prokhorov, U.S.S.R., 1958; (First working model) T. H. Maiman, U.S., 1960.
Lawn mower	Edwin Budding, John Ferrabee, England, 1830-1831.
LCD (liquid crystal display)	Hoffmann-La Roche, Switzerland, 1970. Lightning rod Benjamin Franklin, U.S., c.1760. Benjamin Franklin, U.S., 1752.
Locomotive	(Steam powered) Richard Trevithick, England, 1804; (First practical, due to multiple-fire-tube boiler) George Stephenson, England, 1829; (Largest steam-powered) Machine gun (Hand- cranked multi barrel) Richard J. Gatling, U.S., 1862; (Practical single barrel, belt- fed) Hiram S. Maxim, Anglo-American, 1884.
Measles vaccine	John F. Enders, Thomas Peebles, U.S., 1953.
Microphone	Charles Wheatstone, England, 1827.
Microscope (Compound)	Zacharias Janssen, The Netherlands, 1590; (Electron) Vladimir Zworykin et al., U.S., Canada, Germany, 932-1939.
Microwave oven	Percy Spencer, U.S., 1947.
Motion pictures	Thomas A. Edison, U.S., 1893.
Motorcycle	(Motor tricycle) Edward Butler, England, 1884; (Gasoline-engine motorcycle) Gottlieb Daimler, Germany, 1885.
Neutron	James Chadwick, England, 1932.
Nuclear fission	Otto Hahn, Fritz Strassmann, Germany, 1938.

Nuclear reactor	Enrico Fermi, Italy, et al., 1942.
Oil well	Edwin L. Drake, U.S., 1859.
Ozone	Christian Schonbein, Germany, 1839.
Paper	China, c.100 A.D.
Parachute	Louis S. Lenormand, France, 1783.
Pen (Fountain)	Lewis E. Waterman, U.S., 1884; (Ball-point, for marking on rough surfaces) John H. Loud, U.S., 1888; (Ball-point, for handwriting) Lazlo Biro, Argentina, 1944.
Periodic table	(Arrangement of chemical elements based on periodic law) Dimitri Mendeleev, Russia, 1869.
Phonograph	Thomas A. Edison, U.S., 1877.
Piano (Hammerklavier)	Bartolommeo Cristofori, Italy, 1709; (Pianoforte with sustaining and damper pedals) John Broadwood, England, 1873.
Plate tectonics	Alfred Wegener, Germany, 1912-1915.
Pressure cooker	(Early version) Denis Papin, France, 1679.
Printing (Block)	Japan, c.700; (Movable type) Korea, c.1400; Johann Gutenberg, Germany, c.1450 (Lithography, offset) Aloys Senefelder, Germany, 1796; (Rotary press) Richard Hoe, U.S., 1844; (Linotype) Ottmar Mergenthaler, U.S., 1884.
Proton	Ernest Rutherford, England, 1919.
Pulsars	Antony Hewish and Jocelyn Bell Burnel, England, 1967.
Razor	(Safety, successfully marketed) King Gillette, U.S., 1901; (Electric) Jacob Schick, U.S., 1928, 1931.
Refrigerator	Alexander Twining, U.S., James Harrison, Australia, 1850.
Revolver	Samuel Colt, U.S., 1835.
Richter scale	Charles F. Richter, U.S., 1935.
Rocket (Liquid-fueled)	Robert Goddard, U.S., 1926.

Rubber	(Vulcanization process) Charles Goodyear, U.S., 1839.
Safety pin	Walter Hunt, U.S., 1849.
'Scotch' taps	Richard Drew, U.S., 1929.
Seismograph	(First accurate) John Milne, England, 1880.
Sewing machine	Elias Howe, U.S., 1846; (Continuousstitch) Isaac Singer, U.S., 1851.
Spectrum	(Heterogeneity of light) Sir Isaac Newton, England, 1665-1666.
Spectrum analysis	Gustav Kirchhoff, Robert Bunsen, Germany, 1859.
Stethoscope	Rene Laennec, France, 1819.
Tape recorder	(Magnetic steel tape) Valdemar Poulsen, Denmark, 1899 Teflon DuPont, U.S., 1943.
Telegraph	Samuel E B. Morse, U.S., 1837.
Telephone	Alexander Graham Bell, U.S., 1876.
Telescope	Hans Lipper8hey, The Netherlands, 1608; (Astronomical) Galileo Galilei, Italy, 1609; (Reflecting) Isaac Newton, England, 1668.
Television	(Mechanical disk-scanning method) successfully demonstrated by J.K. Baird, England, G.F. Jenkins, U.S., 1926.
Thermometer	(Open-column) Galileo Galilei, c.1593; (Clinical) Santorio Santorio, Padua, c.1615; (Mercury with Fahrenheit scale) Gabriel D. Fahrenheit, Germany, Alexander Graham Bell 1714.
Tractor	Benjamin Holt, U.S., 1900.
Transistor	John Bardeen, Walter H. Brattain, William B. Shockley, U.S., 1947.
Typewriter	Christopher Sholes, Carlos Glidden, U.S., 1867.

Vaccination	Edward Jenner, England, 1796.
Vacuum cleaner	(Manually operated) Ives W McGaffey, 1869; (Electric) Hubert C. Booth, England, 1901.
Video disk	Philips Co., The Netherlands, 1972.
Wallpaper	Europe, 16th and 17th century Wheel (Cart, solid wood) Mesopotamia, c.3800-3600 B.C. Windmill Persia, c.600.
World Wide Web	(Developed while working at CERN) Tim Berners-Lee, England, 1989.
Zero	India, 600.
Zipper	W L. Judson, U.S., 1891.

RECENT INVENTIONS (2020-2025)

Modern Invention of 2020

The global push towards sustainability led to the development of innovative packaging solutions in 2020. Companies introduced biodegradable materials and reusable packaging to reduce plastic waste. These initiatives have been crucial in addressing environmental concerns and promoting a circular economy.

Modern Invention of 2021

2021 saw significant advancements in robotics, with robots becoming more autonomous and capable of performing complex tasks. Industries such as manufacturing, healthcare, and logistics adopted robotic systems to improve efficiency and safety. These developments have transformed workplaces and have the potential to revolutionize various sectors.

Modern Invention of 2022

In 2022, researchers achieved significant milestones in quantum computing, bringing the technology closer to practical applications. Quantum computers have the potential to solve complex problems in fields like cryptography, materials science, and drug discovery, which are beyond the capabilities of classical computers.

Modern Invention of 2023

The year 2023 marked a significant leap in commercial space travel, with private companies launching regular missions for civilians. These developments have made space more accessible and have sparked interest in space tourism and off-Earth colonization.

Modern Invention of 2024

In 2024 significant inventions emerged across various fields including AI, medicine and technology. Notable examples include Advancements in AI powered tools ,robotic technologies for surgery and assembly and personalized immunotherapy treatments.Additionally breakthrough in renewable energy like carbon capturing microbes and sustainable materials like arognite fiber-optic cables were highlighted.

Modern Invention of 2025

The theoretical potential of Quantum Computers opens upa new line of scientific investigations into quantum mechanics which plums the depth.Over the past year,quantum industry had matured possibly not completely matured but Quantum has moved rapidly from a lab curiosity and marketing tangible for new products like power-ball Quantum, Dishwasher pods and Quantum Storage Bins and organizational solutions.

Modern Invention of 2026

In 2026, modern inventions are expected to focus on the integration of advanced artificial intelligence, biotechnology, and sustainable technologies into everyday life. Major developments include autonomous AI agents capable of independent decision-making, brain–computer interface technologies enhancing human–machine interaction, and next-generation medical innovations such as AI-assisted gene editing and precision diagnostics. Significant progress is also seen in clean energy systems, including solid-state batteries, green hydrogen production, and smart climate-adaptive infrastructure. These inventions indicate a shift toward intelligent, sustainable, and human-centric technological solutions.

❑❑❑

India

10

The Republic of India, commonly known as India, is a sovereign country in South Asia. It is the seventh-largest country by geographical area. It is bounded by the Indian Ocean on the south, the Arabian Sea on the west, and the Bay of Bengal on the east, and has a coastline of over 7000 kilometres.

Capital:	New Delhi
Population:	1,463,865,525 (2025)
Conventional Name:	Republic of India
Local Name:	Republic of India/Bharatiya Ganarajya
Location:	Southern Asia, bordering the Arabian Sea and the Bay of Bengal, between Burma and Pakistan
Chief of Country:	President Droupadi Murmu
Head of Country:	Prime Minister Narendra Modi

LIST OF STATES OF INDIA ALONG WITH THEIR CAPITALS

Here is a list of various states of India along with their capital cities

States	Capital
Andhra Pradesh	Amaravati (*Note: formerly Hyderabad*)
Arunachal Pradesh	Itanagar
Assam	Dispur
Bihar	Patna
Chhattisgarh	Raipur
Goa	Panaji
Gujarat	Gandhinagar
Haryana	Chandigarh
Himachal Pradesh	Shimla

Jammu and Kashmir	Srinagar (Summer), Jammu (Winter)
Jharkhand	Ranchi
Karnataka	Bengaluru
Kerala	Thiruvananthapuram
Madhya Pradesh	Bhopal
Maharashtra	Mumbai
Manipur	Imphal
Meghalaya	Shillong
Mizoram	Aizawl
Nagaland	Kohima
Odisha	Bhubaneswar
Punjab	Chandigarh
Rajasthan	Jaipur
Sikkim	Gangtok
Tamil Nadu	Chennai
Telangana	Hyderabad
Tripura	Agartala
Uttar Pradesh	Lucknow
Uttarakhand	Dehradun
West Bengal	Kolkata

LIST OF UNION TERRITORIES OF INDIA

Here is a list of Union Territories of India along with their capital cities

Union Territories	Headquarters
Andaman and Nicobar Islands	Port Blair
Chandigarh	Chandigarh
Dadra and Nagar Haveli	Silvassa
Daman and Diu	Daman
Jammu and Kashmir	Srinagar (Summer), Jammu (Winter)
National Capital Territory of Delhi	New Delhi
Ladakh	Leh
Lakshadweep	Kavaratti
Puducherry	Puducherry

CHIEF MINISTERS AND GOVERNORS

State	Chief Minister	Governor
Andhra Pradesh	N. Chandrababu Naidu (TDP, NDA)	S. Abdul Nazeer
Arunachal Pradesh	Pema Khandu (BJP, NDA)	K. Trivikram?Parnaik
Assam	Himanta Biswa Sarma (BJP, NDA)	L. Prasad Acharya
Bihar	Nitish Kumar (JD(U), NDA)	Arif Mohammed Khan
Chhattisgarh	Vishnu Deo Sai (BJP, NDA)	Ramen Deka
Goa	Pramod Sawant (BJP, NDA)	P.S. Sreedharan Pillai
Gujarat	Bhupendra Patel (BJP, NDA)	Acharya Devvrat
Haryana	Nayab Singh Saini (BJP, NDA)	Bandaru Dattatreya
Himachal Pradesh	Sukhvinder Singh Sukhu (INC, INDIA)	Shiv Pratap Shukla
Jharkhand	Hemant Soren (JMM, INDIA)	Santosh Gangwar
Karnataka	Siddaramaiah (INC, INDIA)	Thawar Chand Gehlot
Kerala	Pinarayi Vijayan (CPI-M, INDIA)	Rajendra Vishwanath Arlekar
Madhya Pradesh	Mohan Yadav (BJP, NDA)	Mangubhai C. Patel
Maharashtra	Devendra Fadnavis (BJP, NDA)	C.P. Radhakrishnan
Manipur	President's Rule	Ajay Kumar Bhalla
Meghalaya	Conrad Sangma (NPP, NDA)	C.H. Vijayashankar
Mizoram	Lalduhoma (ZPM)	Vijay Kumar Singh
Nagaland	Neiphiu Rio (NDPP, NDA)	La.Ganesan
Odisha	Mohan Charan Majhi (BJP, NDA)	Hari Babu Kambhampati
Punjab	Bhagwant Mann (AAP, INDIA)	Gulab Chand Kataria
Rajasthan	Bhajan Lal Sharma (BJP, NDA)	Haribhau Bagade
Sikkim	Prem Singh Tamang (SKM, NDA)	Om Prakash Mathur
Tamil Nadu	M.K. Stalin (DMK, INDIA)	R.N. Ravi
Telangana	Revanth Reddy (INC, INDIA)	Jishnu Dev Varma
Tripura	Manik Saha (BJP, NDA)	N.Indrasena Reddy
Uttar Pradesh	Yogi Adityanath (BJP, NDA)	Anandiben Patel
Uttarakhand	Pushkar Singh Dhami (BJP, NDA)	Gurmit Singh
West Bengal	Mamata Banerjee (TMC, INDIA)	C.V. Ananda Bose

Union Territories	Chief Ministers	Governor
Andaman & Nicobar Islands	(none)	D.K. Joshi
Chandigarh	(none)	Gulab Chand Kataria
Dadra & Nagar Haveli and Daman & Diu	(none)	Praful Patel
Delhi (NCT)	Rekha Gupta	Vinai Kumar Saxena

Jammu & Kashmir	Omar Abdullah	Manoj Sinha
Ladakh	(none)	B.D. Mishra
Lakshadweep	(none)	Praful Patel
Puducherry	N. Rangaswamy	K.Kailashnathan

PHYSICAL FEATURES

The mainland comprise of four zones:

- The great mountain zone;
- Plains of the Ganga & Indus;
- The desert region, and
- The Southern Peninsula

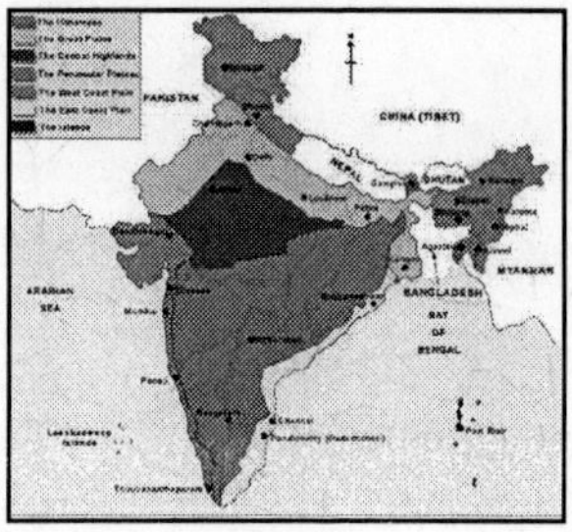

Geological Structure

- The geological regions may be grouped into three regions:
- The Himalayas & their associated group of mountains
- The Indo Ganga Plain
- The Peninsular Shield

Extreme Boundaries

- Northernmost Point – Dafdar in the Taghdumbash Pamir near Beyik Pass in Kanjut in Jammu and Kashmir
- Southernmost Point – Indira Point, Great Nicobar, Andaman and Nicobar Islands
- Westernmost Point – West of Ghuar Mota, Gujarat
- Easternmost Point – Kibithu, Arunachal Pradesh

COUNTRIES HAVING COMMON BOUNDARIES WITH INDIA

- Afghanistan & Pakistan to North West
- China, Bhutan & Nepal to North
- Mayanmar to East
- Bangladesh to East of West Bengal
- Sri Lanka is separated from India by a narrow channel of sea formed by Palk Strait & Gulf of Mayanmar.

Natural Vegetation

The Himalayan region is very rich in natural vegetation. It possess varieties which are found from the tropical to tundra regions. The country, leaving Himalayan region, can be divided in the following three major vegetation:

- The tropical wet evergreen and semi-evergreen forests.
- The tropical deciduous forests.
- The thorn forests and shrubs.

Natural Resources

- Coal (4th largest reserves in the world)
- Manganese
- Bauxite
- Chromite
- Diamonds
- Limestone
- Iron ore
- Mica
- Titanium ore
- Natural gas
- Petroleum
- Arable land

RIVERS

The rivers of India play an important role in the lives of the Indian people. The river systems provide irrigation, potable water, cheap transportation, electricity, and the livelihoods for a large number of people all over the country. All major rivers of India originate from one of the three main watersheds:

1. The Himalaya and the Karakoram ranges
2. Vindhya and Satpura ranges and Chotanagpur plateau in central India
3. Sahyadri or Western Ghats in western India

Most of the rivers pour their waters into the Bay of Bengal; however, some of the rivers whose courses take them through the western part of the country and towards the east of the state of Himachal Pradesh empty into the Arabian Sea.

Ganga

The main river, the holy Ganga forms by the joining of Alaknanda and Andha. Ganga starts from Gangotri glaciers in the Himalayas and flows from Uttar Pradesh and Bihar, and then enters West Bengal and Bangladesh. It ultimately ends in the Bay of Bengal in Bangladesh, where it is known as Padma.

Yamuna

Yamuna traverses 1,375 km from Yamnotri, its Himalayan source in Uttarakhand, to Allahabad in UP, and maintains a seemingly good quality of water till it reaches Wazirabad in Delhi. In Delhi, 15 drains discharge their filthy muck and waste into the river, making it the most polluted river in the country with practically no biologically dissolved oxygen. It runs for 22 km in Delhi and what flows (does not flow) is basically stagnant filth, effluents, sewage and pollutants.

Indus River System

The Indus River originates in the northern slopes of the Kailash range near Lake Mansarovar in Tibet.

Beas

The Beas originates in Bias Kund, lying near the Rohtang pass. It runs past Manali and Kulu, where its beautiful valley is known as the Kulu valley. It joins the Sutlej river near Harika, after being joined by a few tributaries. The total length of the river is 615.

Chenab

The Chenab originates from the confluence of two rivers, the Chandra and the Bhaga, It is also known as the Chandrabhaga in Himachal Pradesh. It runs parallel to the Pir. It enters the plains of Punjab near Akhnur and is later joined by the Jhelum. It is further joined by the Ravi and the Sutlej in Pakistan.

Jhelum

The Jhelum originates in the south-eastern part of Kashmir, in a spring at vernigarp.

Ravi

The Ravi originates near the Rotang pass in the Himalayas and follows a north-westerly course. It turns to the south-west, near Dalhousie, and then cuts a gorge in the Dhaola Dhar range entering the Punjab plain near Madhopur.

It flows as a part of the Indo-Pakistan border for some distance before entering Pakistan and joining the Chenab river.

Sutlej (Satluj)

The Sutlej originates from the Rakas Lake (Rakshas Tal), which is connected to the Manasarovar lake by a stream, in Tibet. It enters Pakistan near Sulemanki, and is later joined by the Chenab. It has a total length of almost 1500 km.

The Brahmaputra River System

The Brahmaputra originates in the Mansarovar lake, also the source of the Indus and the Sutlej. It is slightly longer than the Indus, but most of its course lies outside India. In China, it flows eastward, parallel to the Himalayas by the name of Tsang-Po. Reaching Namcha Barwa (2900m), it takes a U-turn around it and enters India in Arunachal Pradesh and known as Dihang.

The Narmada River System

The Narmada' or Nerbudda is a river in central India.It forms the traditional boundary between North India and South India, and is a total of 1,289 km (801 mi) long. Of the major rivers of peninsular India, only the Narmada, the Tapti and the Mahi run from east to west. Narmada originates from Amarkantak.

The Taapi River System

The Taapi is a river of central India. It is one of the major rivers of peninsular India with the length of around 724 km, It rises in the eastern Satpura Range of southern Madhya Pradesh state, before emptying into the Gulf of Cambay of the Arabian Sea, in the State of Gujarat.

The Godavari River System

The river with second longest course within India, Godavari is often referred to as the Vriddh (Old) Ganga or the Dakshin (South) Ganga. The river is about 1,450 km (900 mi) long.

It rises at Trimbakeshwar, near Nasik and Mumbai (formerly Bombay) in Maharashtra around 380 km distance from the Arabian Sea, and empties into the Bay of Bengal.

The Krishna River System

The Krishna is one of the longest rivers of India (about 1300 km in length). It originates at Mahabaleswar in Maharashtra and meets the sea in the Bay of Bengal at Hamasaladeevi in Andhra Pradesh. The Krishna River flows through the states of Maharashtra, Karnataka and Andhra Pradesh.

The Kaveri River System

The Kaveri (also spelled Cauvery or Kavery) is one of the great rivers of India and is considered sacred by the Hindus.this is the [holy river] of south Indians . birth place of river kaveri called as [Dakshin Kashi] (god shiva temple called [Bhagandeshwar] at [Bhagamandala] and caveri temple at [talakaveri]. It empties into the Bay of Bengal.

The Mahanadi River System

The Mahanadi River flows slowly for 560 miles (900 km) and has an estimated drainage area of 51,000 square miles (132,100 square km). It deposits more silt than almost any other river in the Indian subcontinent.

MOUNTAINS

A great arc of mountains, composed of the Himalaya, Hindu Kush, and Patkai ranges, define the Indian subcontinent. These mountains were formed by the ongoing tectonic collision of the Indian Plate with the Eurasian Plate which started some 50 million years ago. These mountain ranges are home to some of the world's tallest mountains and act as a natural barrier to cold polar winds. India has nine major mountain ranges having peaks of over 1,000 m (3,281 ft). The Himalayas are the only mountain ranges to have snow-capped peaks. These ranges are:

- Aravalli Range
- Himalayas
- Vindhya Range
- Satpura Range
- Kunlun
- Eastern Ghats
- Patkai
- Western Ghats (Sahyadri)
- Karakoram

CONSTITUTION OF INDIA

The Constitution of India was drafted by the Constituent Assembly. It held its first sitting on the 9th December, 1946. It reassembled on the 14th

August, 1947, as the sovereign Constituent Assembly for the Dominion of India. The proposed Constitution had been outlined by various committees of the Assembly like:

- Union Constitution Committee
- The Union Powers Committee
- Committee on Fundamental Rights.

It was after a general discussion on the reports of these Committees that the Assembly appointed a Drafting Committee on the 29th August, 1947. The Drafting Committee, under the Chairmanship of Dr. B. R. Ambedkar, embodied the decision of the Assembly with alternative and additional proposals in the form of a 'Draft Constitution of India which was published in February, 1948.

After several sessions the consideration of the clauses or second reading was completed by the 17th October, 1949. The Constituent Assembly again sat on the 14th November, 1949, for the third reading and finished it on the 26th November, 1949, on which date the Constitution received the signature of the President of the Assembly and was declared as passed.

PREAMBLE OF INDIA

WE, THE PEOPLE OF INDIA, having solemnly resolved to constitute India into a **SOVEREIGN SOCIALIST SECULAR DEMOCRATIC REPUBLIC**

and to secure to all its citizens:

JUSTICE, social, economic and political;

LIBERTY of thought, expression, belief, faith and worship;

EQUALITY of status and of opportunity; and to promote among them all;

FRATERNITY assuring the dignity of the individual and the unity and integrity of the Nation;

IN OUR CONSTITUENT ASSEMBLY this twenty-sixth day of November, 1949, do **HEREBY ADOPT, ENACT AND GIVE TO OURSELVES THIS CONSTITUTION**.

Purpose of Having a Preamble

The Preamble to our Constitution serves two purposes:

It indicates the source from which the Constitution derives its authority; It also states the objects, which the Constitution seeks to establish and promote.

The Preamble seeks to establish what **Mahatma Gandhi** described as "The India of my Dreams," an India in which the poorest shall feel that it is their country in whose making they have an effective voice; an India in which all communities shall live in perfect harmony. There can be no room in such an India for the curse of untouchability or the curse of

Intoxicating drinks and drugs. Women will enjoy as the same rights as men."

Fundamental Rights

The Fundamental Rights embodied in the Indian Constitution Act as a guarantee that all Indian citizens and will lead their lives in peace as long as they live in Indian democracy. These civil liberties take precedence over any other law of the land. They include individual rights common to mostliberaldemocracies, andequalitybeforethelaw, freedomofspeech and expression, freedom of association and peaceful assembly, freedom of religion, and the right to constitutional remedies for the protection of civil rights such as habeas corpus. We have defined the six fundamental rights as per the Constitution of India:

- Right to Equality
- Right to Particular Freedom
- Cultural and Educational Rights
- Right to Freedom of Religion
- Right Against Exploitation, and
- Right to Constitutional Remedies

Fundamental Duties

It shall be the duty of every citizens of India:

- To abide by the Constitution and respect its ideals and institutions, the National Flag and the National Anthem;
- To cherish and follow the noble ideals which inspired our national struggle for freedom;

- To uphold and protect the sovereignty, unity and integrity of India;
- To defend the country and render national service when called upon to do so;
- To promote harmony and the spirit of common brotherhood amongstallthe peopleof Indiatranscendingreligious, linguisticand regional or sectional diversities; to renounce practices derogatory to the dignity of women;
- To value and preserve the rich heritage of our composite culture;
- To protect and improve the natural environment including forests, lakes, rivers and wild life, and to have compassion for living creatures;
- To develop the scientific temper, humanism and the spirit of inquiry and reform;
- To safeguard public property and to abjure violence;
- To strive towards excellence in all spheres of individual and collective activity so that the nation constantly rises to higher levels of endeavour and achievement.

PUBLIC HOLIDAYS

National holidays India 2011 – The National public holidays 2011 in India are fixed and commemorate the major non-religious and are never subject to any change.

India Republic Day - Wednesday, 26 January 2011

Independence Day (Celebrates India Independence) - Monday, 15 August 2011

Gandhi Jayanti (Mahatma Gandhi's Birthday) - Sunday, 2 October 2011

Religious India holidays 2016

Every state and region observes local festivals and depending on these the holiday list is prepared. Here is the list of declared government public holidays in India for 2016 –

Makar Sankranti	15th January, 2016
Vasant Panchami – Saraswati Puja	February 13, 2016
Shivratri	March 7, 2016
Dhulandi Holi	March 24. 2016

Ram Navami	April 15, 2016
Hanuman Jayanti	April 22, 2016
Vyas Purnima, Guru Purnima	July 19
Raksha Bandhan	August 18, 2016
Sri Krishna Janmashtami	August 25
Ganesh Chaturthi	September 5
Bishwakarma Puja	September 17
Durga Ashtami	October 9
Vijaya Dashami – Dussehra	October 11
Karva Chouth	October 18
Dhanteras	October 28
Diwali	October 30
Bhau Beej	November 1
Chath Puja	November 6
Christmas Day	25 December

NATIONAL ELECTION

Rajya Sabha Members

Rajya Sabha members are indirectly elected, and are almost entirely elected by Members of Assembly of individual states (Vidhan Sabhas), while 12 members are nominated by the President of India, usually with the advice and consent from the Prime Minister of India.

President of India

The President of India is indirectly elected to a 5 year term. The electoral college is used where the members of the Parliament of both the Lok Sabha and the Rajya Sabha, and the Members of Legislative Assemblies (Vidhan Sabha from all states and territories of India) cast their vote.

The Election Commission

Elections in India are conducted by the Election Commission of India, the authority created under the Constitution. It is a well established convention that once the election process commences; no courts intervene until the results are declared by the Election Commission.

Parliament

Parliament is the supreme legislative body of India. The Indian Parliament comprises of the President and the two Houses-Lok Sabha (House of the People) and Rajya Sabha (Council of States). The President has the power to summon and prorogue either House of Parliament or to dissolve Lok Sabha.

Council of Ministers (According to Parliament held in May 2024)

1. Cabinet Ministers
2. Ministers of State with Independent Charge
3. Ministers of State Cabinet Ministers

S. N.	Portfolio	Name of Minister
Union Council of Ministers		
1	Personnel, Public Grievances and Pensions, Department of Atomic Energy, Department of Space, All important policy issues and All other portfolios not allocated to any Minister	**Narendra Modi** 
Cabinet Ministers		
1	Home Affairs	Amit Shah
2	External Affairs	Subrahmanyam Jaishankar
3	Finance, Corporate Affairs	Nirmala Sitharaman
4	Urban Development, Housing and Urban Poverty Alleviation, Information & Broadcasting	M. Venkaiah Naidu
5	Road Transport and Highways, Shipping	Nitin Jairam Gadkari
6	Defence	Rajnath Singh
7	Railways	Ashwini Vaishnaw
8	Statistics & Programme Implementation	Rao Inderjit Singh
9	Water Resources, River Development and Ganga Rejuvenation	Shri C. R. Patil
10	Consumer Affairs, Food and Public Distribution	Pralhad Joshi
11	Micro, Small and Medium Enterprises	Jitan Ram Manjhi

12	Women and Child Development	Annpurna Devi
13	Chemicals and Fertilizers	Shri Jagat Prakash Nadda
14	Law & Justice, Electronics & Information Technology	Arjun Ram Meghwal
15	Health and Family Welfare	Prataprao Jadhav
16	Civil Aviation Naidu	Kinjarapu Rammohan
17	Heavy Industries and Public Enterprises	H. D. Kumaraswamy
18	Food Processing Industries	Chirag Paswan
19	Rural Development, Panchayati Raj, Drinking Water and Sanitation	Lalan Singh
20	Heavy Industries & Steel	H. D. Kumaraswamy
21	Tribal Affairs	Jual Oram
22	Agriculture & Farmers Welfare	Shri Shivraj Singh Chouhan
23	Social Justice and Empowerment	Virendra Kumar
24	Textiles	Giriraj Singh
25	Science and Technology, Earth Sciences	Dr. Jitendra Singh
26	Human Resource Development	Shri Dharmendra Pradhan
27	Ministry of Coal	G. Kishan Reddy
28	Parliamentary Affairs	Shri Kiren Rijiju

Ministers of State with Independent Charge

S. N.	Portfolio	Name of Minister
1	Planning (Independent Charge), Urban Development, Housing & Urban Poverty Alleviation	Rao Inderjit Singh
2	Labour and Employment (Independent Charge)	Bhupender Yadav
3	Skill Development & Entrepreneurship (Independent Charge)	Jayant Chaudhary
4	Youth Affairs and Sports (Independent Charge), Water Resources, River Development & Ganga Rejuvenation	Anurag Thakur
5	AAYUSH (Independent Charge)	Sarbananda Sonowal

6	Petroleum and Natural Gas (Independent Charge)	Hardeep Singh Puri
7	Power (Independent Charge), Coal (Independent Charge), New and Renewable Energy (Independent Charge), Mines (Independent Charge)	Manohar Lal Khattar
8	Development of North Eastern Region (Independent Charge), Prime Minister's Office, Personnel, Public Grievances & Pensions, Department of Atomic Energy, Department of Space	Dr. Jitendra Singh
9	Commerce and Industry (Independent Charge)	Piyush Goyal
10	Culture (Independent Charge), Tourism (Independent Charge)	G. Kishan Reddy
11	Communications (Independent Charge), Railways	Ashwini Vaishnaw
12	Environment, Forest and Climate Change (Independent Charge)	Bhupender Yadav
13	Minority Affairs (Independent Charge), Parliamentary Affairs	Mukhtar Abbas Naqvi

Ministers of State

S. N.	Portfolio	Name of Minister
1	External Affairs	S. Jaishankar
2	Finance	Nirmala Sitharaman
3	Health & Family Welfare	J. P. Nadda
4	Agriculture & Farmers Welfare, Parliamentary Affairs	Shivraj Singh Chouhan
5	Social Justice & Empowerment	Dr. Virendra Kumar (Cabinet) Shri Ratan Lal Kataria
6	Rural Development	Shivraj Singh Chouhan

7	Micro, Small & Medium Enterprises	Jitan Ram Manjhi
8	Micro, Small & Medium Enterprises	Shri Prataprao Jadhav (I/C)
9	Home Affairs	Amit Shah
10	Drinking Water & Sanitation	C. R. Patil
11	Railways	Ashwini Vaishnaw
12	Agriculture & Farmers Welfare, Panchayati Raj	Shri Kailash Choudhary
13	External Affairs	(Merged under Meenakshi Lekhi)
14	Education (formerly HRD)	Dharmendra Pradhan
15	Road Transport & Highways, Shipping	Nitin Gadkari
16	Home Affairs Nityanand Rai)	(MoS, mainly handled by
17	Social Justice & Empowerment	Shri Ratan Lal Kataria
18	Tribal Affairs	Jual Oram
19	Water Resources, River Development & Ganga Rejuvenation Choudhary	Shri V. Somanna, Shri Raj Bhushan
20	Steel	H. D. Kumaraswamy
21	Agriculture & Farmers Welfare	Shri Ram Nath Thakur
22	Science & Technology, Earth Sciences	Shri Dr. Jitendra Singh (I/C)
23	Civil Aviation	K. Rammohan Naidu
24	Information & Broadcasting	Ashwini Vaishnaw
25	Heavy Industries & Public Enterprises	Shri Baijayant "Jay" Panda
26	Food Processing Industries	Chirag Paswan
27	Social Justice & Empowerment	Shri Ratan Lal Kataria
28	Finance, Corporate Affairs	Shri Dr. Bhagwat Karad
29	Education (formerly HRD)	Dr. Subhas Sarkar
30	Textiles	Giriraj Singh
31	Women & Child Development	Annapurna Devi
32	Road Transport & Highways, Shipping, Chemicals & Fertilizers	Shri Mansukh L. Mandaviya (Cabinet)
33	Health & Family Welfare	Smt. Anupriya Patel (Cabinet)
34	Consumer Affairs, Food & Public Distribution	Shri C.R. Chaudhary (Cabinet)

35	Law & Justice, Electronics & Information Technology	Shri P.P. Chaudhary (Cabinet)
36	Defence	Rajnath Singh

List of Presidents Since Freedom

Dr. Rajendra Prasad	Jan. 26,1950 - May 13, 1962
Dr. S. Radhakrishnan	May 13, 1962 - May 13, 1967
Dr. Zakir Hussain	May 13, 1967 - August 24, 1969
Shri Varahagiri Venkata Giri	August 24, 1969 - August 24, 1974
Shri Fakhruddin Ali Ahmed	August 24, 1974 - February 11, 1977
Shri Neelam Sanjiva Reddy	July 25, 1977 - July 25, 1982
Shri Giani Zail Singh	July 25, 1982—July 25, 1987
Shri R. Venkataraman	July 25, 1987- July 25, 1992
Dr.S.D. Sharma	July 25, 1992 - July 25, 1997
Shri K R Narayanan	July 25, 1997 - 2002
Dr.A P J Addul Kalam	July 25, 2002 - 2007
Pratibha Patil	July 25, 2007 - 2012
Pranab Mukherjee	25 July 2012 to 25 July 2017
Ramnath Kovind	25 July 2017 to 25 July 2022
Droupadi Murmu	25 July 2022 to Incumbent

List of Vice Presidents Since Freedom

Basappa Danappa Jatti	31 August, 1974 Till 30 August, 1979
Muhammad Hidayat Ullah	31 August, 1979 Till 30 August, 1984
Ramaswamy Venkataraman	31 August, 1984 Till 27 July, 1987
Dr.Shanker Dayal Sharma	3 September, 1987 Till 24 July, 1992
Kocheril Raman Narayanan	21 August, 1992 Till 24 July, 1997
Krishan Kant	21 August, 1997 Till 27 July, 2002
Bhairon Singh Shekhawat	19 August, 2002 Till 21 July, 2007
Hamid Ansari	11 August 2012 to 11August 2017.
M.Venkaiah Naidu	11 August 2017 to 11 August 2022
Jagdeep Dhankhar	11 August 2022 to 21 July 2025
C. P. Radhakrishnan	12 Sep 2025 to incumbent

List of Prime Ministers Since Freedom

Shri Jawaharlal Nehru	August 15, 1947 - May 27, 1964
Shri Gulzari Lal Nanda	May 27, 1964 – 9 June, 1964
Shri Lal Bahadur Shastri	June 9, 1964 - January 11, 1966
Shri Gulzari Lal Nanda	January 11, 1966 - January 24, 1966
Shrimati Indira Gandhi	January 24, 1966 - March 24, 1977
Shri Morarji Desai	March 24, 1977 - July 28, 1979
Shri Charan Singh	July 28, 1979 - January 14, 1980
Shrimati Indira Gandhi	January 14, 1980 - October 31, 1984
Shri Rajiv Gandhi	October 31, 1984 - December 1, 1989
Shri Vishwanath Pratap Singh	Dec. 2, 1989 - November 10, 1990
Shri Chandra Shekhar	November 10, 1990 - June 21, 1991
Shri P.V. Narasimha Rao	June 21, 1991 - May 16, 1996
Shri Atal Behari Vajpayee	May 16, 1996 - 1 June 1996
Shri H. D. Deve Gowda	1 June 1996 - 12 April 1997
Shri Inder Kumar Gujral	21 April 1997 - 19 Mar 1998
Shri Atal Behari Vajpayee	19 Mar 1998 - May 21 2004
Dr Manmohan Singh	May 22, 2004 - 25 May 2014
Narender Modi	May 26, 2014 till date

POPULATION

India is the **most populated country in the world**, surpassing China in **2023**, according to the United Nations. As of **2025**, India's population is estimated to be over **1.43 billion**. Population growth has long been a critical issue, closely linked with challenges such as **poverty**, **illiteracy**, **unemployment**, and **pressure on infrastructure and natural resources**.

Hindus form the majority at around **79.8%**, followed by Muslims, who constitute approximately **14.2%** of the population, making India home to one of the **world's largest Muslim populations**. Other religious groups include **Christians (2.3%)**, **Sikhs (1.7%)**, **Buddhists (0.7%)**, **Jains (0.4%)**, and **Parsis**, among others.

According to the **2011 Census**, the population was **1.21 billion**, with **Scheduled Castes (SCs)** accounting for **16.6%** and **Scheduled Tribes (STs)** making up **8.6%**. The **annual population growth rate** has slowed in recent years and is now estimated at approximately **1.0% or lower** as of 2025.

Structure :

0-14 years: 25.68% (male 183,695,000/female 166,295,000) (2021)

15-64 years: 64.3% (male 472,653,000/female 447,337,000) (2021)

65 years and over: 6.83% (male 44,275,000/female 48,751,000) (2021 est.)

Median Age :

Total: 28.2 years

Male: 29.05 years

Female: 29.87 years (2021 est.)

Population Growth Rate: +0.89% (2023)

Birth Rate : 16.15 births/1,000 population (2024 est.)

Death Rate : 9.1 deaths/1,000 population (July 2024 est.)

Net Migration Rate : -0.68 (2024) migrant(s)/1,000 population (2024 est.)

Urbanization :

Urban population: 38% of total population (2023)

Sex Ratio :

At birth: 1.1 male(s)/female

Under 15 years: 1.11 male(s) / female 15-64 years: 1.06 male(s) / female

65 years and over: 0.85 male(s) / female

Total population: 1.06 male(s)/female (2023 est.)

Life expectancy at Birth :

Total population: 72.03 years Male: 70.52 years

Female: 73.67 years (2023 est.)

LANGUAGES IN INDIA

India is very rich in languages. There are uncountable number of languages and dialects being spoken in India. A mixture of 30 different languages have been identified along with 2000 dialects.

Official Languages of India

There are two languages used by the central administration of India.

They are:

- Hindi
- English

Recognized National Languages of India

There are a total of 22 languages scheduled for official use. They are as follows:

Languages	Number of Speakers (in million)	States where it is Official Language
Assamese	13	Assam
Bengali	70	Tripura and West Bengal Assam
Bodo		Assam
Malayalam	30	Kerala and Lakshadweep
Manipuri or Meithei	1.2	Manipur
Marathi	63	Maharashtra
Nepali	1	Sikkim
Oriya	28	Orissa
Punjabi	23	Punjab, second official language of Delhi
Sanskrit	0.1	
Sindhi	2.1	
Tamil	53	Tamil Nadu and Puducherry
Telugu	66	Andhra Pradesh
Urdu	43	Jammu and Kashmir

LIST OF BANKS IN INDIA

Central Bank

Reserve Bank of India - Central bank and supreme monetary authority Nationalised banks (Public Sector)

- Allahabad Bank
- Andhra Bank
- Bank of Baroda
- Bank of India
- Bank of Maharashtra
- Canara Bank
- Central Bank of India
- Corporation Bank
- Dena Bank
- IDBI Bank

- Indian Bank
- Oriental Bank of Commerce
- Syndicate Bank
- UCO Bank
- Vijaya Bank
- Indian Overseas Bank
- Punjab National Bank
- Union Bank of India
- United Bank of India
- SBI (State Bank of India)

SBI & associates (Nationalised)

- State Bank of India
- State Bank of Hyderabad
- State Bank of Patiala
- State Bank of Bikaner & Jaipur
- State Bank of Mysore
- State Bank of Travancore
- State Bank of Indore - (merged with SBI in 2010)
- State Bank of Saurashtra - (merged with SBI in 2008)

Private Banks

- Axis Bank (Formerly UTI Bank)
- ICICI Bank (Siddhashila)
- Karnataka Bank
- IndusInd Bank
- ING Vysya Bank
- HDFC Bank
- Kotak Mahindra Bank
- Yes Bank
- The Nainital Bank Ltd.

Scheduled Urban Co-operative Banks

Bank	Main Location
Rani Laxmibai Urban Co-op Bank,	Jhansi
Ahmedabad Mercantile Co-op Bank Ltd.	Ahmedabad
Kalupur Commercial Coop.Bank Ltd.	Kalupur
Madhavpura Mercantile Co-op Bank Ltd.	Madhavpur
Mehsana Urban Co-op Bank Ltd.	Mehsana
Nutan Nagarik Sahakari Bank Ltd.	Ahmedabad
Rajkot Nagarik Sahakari Bank Ltd.	Rajkot
Almora Urban Co-operative Bank ltd.	Almora
South Indian Bank	Tirichur
Sardar Bhiladwala Pardi Peoples Co-op Bank Ltd.	Bulsar
Surat Peoples Co-op Bank Ltd.	Surat

Amanath Co-operative Bank Ltd.	Bangalore
Andhra Pradesh Mahesh Co-op Urban Bank Ltd.	Andhra Pradesh
Charminar Co-op.Urban Bank Ltd.	Hyderabad
Vasavi Coop Urban Bank Limited.	Hyderabad
Indian Mercantile Co-op Bank Ltd.	Lucknow
Kallappanna Awade Ichalkaranji Janata Sahakari Bank Ltd.	Ichalkaranji
Abhyudaya Co-operative Bank Ltd.	Mumbai
Bangalore City Cooperative bank.	Bengaluru
Bassein Catholic Co-operative Bank Limited.	Vasai
Bharat Co-operative Bank (Mumbai) Ltd.	Mumbai
Bharati Sahakari Bank Limited.	Pune
Bombay Mercantile Co-operative Bank Limited.	Mumbai
Citizens' Credit Co-operative Bank Ltd.	Dadar
Cosmos Co-operative Urban Bank Ltd.	Pune
Dombivli Nagari Sahakari Bank Ltd.	Dombivli
Goa Urban Co-operative Bank Limited.	Goa
Greater Bombay Co-operative Bank Limited.	Mumbai
Jalgaon Janata Sahakari Bank Ltd.	Jalgaon
Janakalyan Sahakari Bank Ltd.	Mumbai
Janalaxmi Co-operative Bank Ltd.	Mumbai
Janata Sahakari Bank Ltd.	Pune
The Karnataka State Co-operative Apex Bank Ltd	Bengaluru
Kalyan Janata Sahakari Bank Ltd.	Kalyan
Karad Urban Co-operative Bank Ltd.	Karad
Mahanagar Co-operative Bank Ltd.	Mumbai
Mapusa Urban Co-operative Bank of Goa Ltd.	Mapusa Nagar
Urban Co-operative Bank Ltd.	Ahmednagar
Nasik Merchant's Co-operative Bank Ltd.	Nasik
New India Co-operative Bank Ltd.	Mumbai
NKGSB Co-operative Bank Ltd.	Mumbai
Parsik Janata Sahakari Bank Ltd.	Thane
Pravara Sahakari Bank Ltd.	Ahmednagar
Punjab & Maharashtra Co-operative Bank Ltd.	Mumbai
Rupee Co-operative Bank Ltd.	Pune

Sangli Urban Co-operative Bank Ltd.	Sangli
Saraswat Co-operative Bank Ltd.	Mumbai
Shamrao Vithal Co-operative Bank Ltd.	Mumbai
Solapur Janata Sahakari Bank Ltd.	Solapur
Thane Bharat Sahakari Bank Ltd.	Thane
Thane Janata Sahakari Bank Ltd.	Thane
The Kapol Co-operative Bank Ltd.	Mumbai
Zoroastrian Co-operative Bank Ltd.	Mumbai
Nagpur Nagrik Sahakari Bank Ltd.	Nagpur
Shikshak Sahakari Bank Ltd.	Nagpur
The Akola Janata Com.Co-operative Bank Ltd.	Akola
The Akola Urban Co-operative Bank Ltd.	Akola
The Khamgaon Urban Co-operative Bank Ltd.	Khamgaon
Cuttack Gramya Bank.	Cuttack

Non-Scheduled Urban Co-operative Banks

Bank	Main Location
Janaseva Sahakari Bank Ltd.,	Pune
Vishweshwar Sahakari Bank Ltd.,	Pune
Sadhna Sahakari Bank Ltd.,	Pune
Sanmitra Sahakari Bank Ltd.	Pune

Foreign Banks in India

- ABN AMRO Bank
- Royal Bank of Scotland
- Abu Dhabi Commercial Bank Ltd
- American Express Bank
- Antwerp Diamond Bank
- Arab Bangladesh Bank
- Bank International Indonesia
- Bank of America
- Bank of Bahrain & Kuwait
- Bank of Ceylon
- Bank of Novascotia
- Bank of Tokyo Mitsubishi UFJ
- Barclays Bank
- BNP Paribas
- Calyon Bank
- China Trust Commercial Bank
- Citibank
- DBS Bank
- Deutsche Bank

- J P Morgan Chase Bank
- Mashreq Bank
- Oman International Bank
- Société Générale
- Standard Chartered Bank
- UBS
- Krung Thai Bank
- Mizuho Corporate Bank
- Shinhan Bank
- Sonali Bank
- State Bank of Mauritius
- VTB
- HSBC (Hongkong & Shanghai Banking Corporation)

AWARDS AND HONOURS IN INDIA

Padma Vibhushan Recipients

Name	Field	Place
2025		
Duvvur Nageshwar Reddy	Medicine	Telangana
Justice (R.) Jagdish Singh Khehar	Public Affairs	Chandigarh
Kumudini Rajnikant Lakhia	Arts	Gujarat
Lakshminarayana Subramaniam	Arts	Karnataka
M.T. Vasudevan Nair (Posthumous)	Literature & Education	Kerala
Osamu Suzuki (Posthumous)	Trade & Industry	Japan
Sharda Sinha (Posthumous)	Arts	Bihar
2024		
Ms. Vyjayantimala Bali	(Art)	Tamil Nadu
Shri Konidela Chiranjeevi	(Art)	Andhra Pradesh
Shri M Venkaiah Naidu	(Public Affairs)	Andhra Pradesh
Shri Bindeshwar Pathak	(Social Work)	Bihar
Ms. Padma Subrahmanyam	(Art)	Tamil Nadu
2023		
Balkrishna Doshi (Posthumous)	Architecture / Others	Gujarat
Dilip Mahalanabis (Posthumous)	Medicine	West Bengal
Mulayam Singh Yadav (Posthumous)	Public Affairs	Uttar Pradesh
Zakir Hussain	Arts	Maharashtra
S. M. Krishna	Public Affairs	Karnataka
Srinivas Varadhan	Science & Engineering	USA

2022		
Ms. Prabha Atre	Art	Maharashtra
Shri Radheyshyam Khemka (Posthumous)	Literature and Education	Uttar Pradesh
General Bipin Rawat (Posthumous)		Civil Service
Uttarakhand		
Shri Kalyan Singh (Posthumous)	Public Affairs	Uttar Pradesh
2021		
Narinder Singh Kapany	Science & Engineering	Punjab
Wahiduddin Khan	Others	Delhi
B. B. Lal	Others	Delhi
Sudarshan Sahoo	Arts	Odisha
2020		
George Fernandes (Posthumous)	Public Affairs	Bihar
Arun Jaitley (Posthumous)	Public Affairs	Delhi
Sir Anerood Jugnauth	Public Affairs	Mauritius
M. C. Mary Kom	Sports	Manipur
Chhannulal Mishra	Arts	Uttar Pradesh
Sushma Swaraj (Posthumous)	Public Affairs	Delhi

PADMA BHUSHAN RECIPIENTS

Name	Field	Place
2025		
A. Surya Prakash	Literature & Education	Karnataka
Anant Nag	Arts	Karnataka
Bibek Debroy	Literature & Education	Delhi
Jatin Goswami	Arts	Assam
Jose Chacko Periappuram	Medicine	Kerala
Kailash Nath Dikshit	Others	Delhi
Manohar Joshi	Public Affairs	Maharashtra
Nalli Kuppuswami Chetti	Trade & Industry	Tamil Nadu
Nandamuri Balakrishna	Arts	Andhra Pradesh
P. R. Sreejesh	Sports	Kerala

Pankaj Patel	Trade & Industry	Gujarat
Pankaj Udhas	Arts	Maharashtra
Ram Bahadur Rai	Literature & Education	Uttar Pradesh
Sadhvi Rithambara	Social Work	Uttar Pradesh
Ajith Kumar	Arts	Tamil Nadu
Shekhar Kapur	Arts	Maharashtra
Shobana	Arts	Kerala
Sushil Kumar Modi	Public Affairs	Bihar
Vinod Dham	Science & Engineering	United States

2024

Ms. M Fathima Beevi	(Public Affairs)	Kerala
Shri Hormusji N Cama	(Literature & Education)	Maharashtra
Shri Mithun Chakraborty	(Art)	West Bengal
Shri Sitaram Jindal	(Trade & Industry)	Karnataka
Shri Young Liu	(Trade & Industry)	Taiwan
Shri Ashwin Balachand Mehta	(Medicine)	Maharashtra
Shri Satyabrata Mookherjee	(Public Affairs)	West Bengal
Shri Ram Naik	(Public Affairs)	Maharashtra
Shri Tejas Madhusudan Patel	(Medicine)	Gujarat
Shri Olanchery Rajagopal	(Public Affairs)	Kerala
Shri Dattatray Ambadas Mayaloo alias Rajdutt	(Art)	Maharashtra
Shri Togdan Rinpoche	(Others - Spiritualism)	Ladakh
Shri Pyarelal Sharma	(Art)	Maharashtra
Shri Chandreshwar Prasad Thakur	(Medicine)	Bihar
Ms. Usha Uthup	(Art)	West Bengal
Shri Vijaykanth	(Art)	Tamil Nadu
Shri Kundan Vyas	(Literature & Education - Journalism)	Maharashtra

2023

S. L. Bhyrappa	Literature & Education	Karnataka
Kumar Mangalam Birla	Trade & Industry	Maharashtra

Deepak Dhar	Science & Engineering	Maharashtra
Vani Jairam	Arts	Tamil Nadu
Chinna Jeeyar	Others	Telangana
Suman Kalyanpur	Arts	Maharashtra
Kapil Kapoor	Literature & Education	Delhi
Sudha Murthy	Social Work	Karnataka
Kamlesh Patel	Others	Telangana

2022

Ghulam Nabi Azad	Public Affairs	J&K
Gurmeet Bawa	Arts	Punjab
Natarajan Chandrasekaran	Trade & Industry	Maharashtra
Madhur Jaffrey	Others	United States
Devendra Jhajharia	Sports	Rajasthan
Rashid Khan	Arts	Uttar Pradesh
Rajiv Mehrishi	Civil Service	Rajasthan
Satya Nadella	Trade & Industry	United States
Sundar Pichai	Trade & Industry	United States
Cyrus S. Poonawalla	Trade & Industry	Maharashtra
Sanjaya Rajaram	Science & Engineering	Mexico
Pratibha Ray	Literature & Education	Odisha
Swami Sachchidanand	Literature & Education	Gujarat
Vashishth Tripathi	Literature & Education	Uttar Pradesh
Krishna Ella/Suchitra Ella	Trade & Industry	Telangana
Victor Banerjee	Arts	West Bengal

2021

K. S. Chithra	Arts	Kerala
Tarun Gogoi	Public Affairs	Assam
Chandrashekhara Kambara	Literature & Education	Karnataka
Nripendra Misra	Civil Service	Uttar Pradesh
Ram Vilas Paswan	Public Affairs	Bihar
Keshubhai Patel	Public Affairs	Gujarat
Kalbe Sadiq	Others	Uttar Pradesh
Rajnikant Shroff	Trade & Industry	Maharashtra
Tarlochan Singh	Public Affairs	Haryana

2020

Sri M	Others	Kerala
Syed Muazzem Ali	Public Affairs	Bangladesh
Muzaffar Hussain Baig	Public Affairs	J&K
Ajoy Chakrabarty	Arts	West Bengal
Manoj Das	Literature & Education	Puducherry
Balkrishna Vithaldas Doshi	Others	Gujarat
Krishnammal Jagannathan	Social Work	Tamil Nadu
S. C. Jamir	Public Affairs	Nagaland
Anil Prakash Joshi	Social Work	Uttarakhand
Tsering Landol	Medicine	Ladakh
Anand Mahindra	Trade & Industry	Maharashtra
N. R. Madhava Menon	Public Affairs	Kerala
Manohar Parrikar	Public Affairs	Goa
Jagdish Sheth	Literature & Education	United States
P. V. Sindhu	Sports	Telangana
Venu Srinivasan	Trade & Industry	Maharashtra
Sumitra Mahajan	Public Affairs	Madhya Pradesh

PADMASHRI

The award is given for distinguished service in any field including service rendered by the Government servants.

Padma Shri 2025 winners: Unsung heroes

1. Arijit Singh, Art
2. Sharda Sinha, Art (Posthumous)
3. Radha Bhatt, Social Work
4. Anil Kumar Boro, Literature and Education
5. Ajay V. Bhatt, Science and Engineering
6. Vasudevan Nair, Art (Posthumous)
7. Pandit Ram Mandavi, Art
8. R. Ashwin, Sports
9. S. Ajith Kumar, Sports
10. Shekhar Kapur, Art
11. Anant Nag, Art

12. Harvinder Singh, Sports
13. Satyapal Singh, Sports
14. Arunoday Saha, Literature and Education
15. Arvind Sharma, Literature and Education

Padma Shri 2024 winners: Unsung heroes

1. Parbati Baruah - India's first female elephant mahout
2. Chami Murmu - Renowned tribal environmentalist
3. Sangthankima - Social worker from Mizoram
4. Jageshwar Yadav - Tribal welfare worker
5. Gurvinder Singh - Divyang social worker from Sirsa
6. Sathyanarayana Beleri - Rice farmer from Kasaragod
7. Dukhu Majhi - Tribal environmentalist from Sindri village
8. K Chellammal - Organic farmer from Andaman
9. Hemchand Manjhi - Medicinal practitioner from Narayanpur
10. Yanung Jamoh Lego - Herbal medicine expert from Arunachal Pradesh
11. Rohan Machanda Bopanna, Sports
12. Nirmal Rishi, Art
13. Harbinder Singh, Sports

Padma Shri 2023 winners: Unsung heroes

1. Nalini Parthasarathi, Medicine
2. Ramesh Patange, Literature & Education
3. Krishna Patel, Art
4. V. P. Appukuttan Poduval, Social Work
5. Kapil Dev Prasad, Art
6. S R D Prasad, Sports
7. Bakshi Ram, Science & Engineering
8. Cheruvayal K Raman, Agriculture
9. Manoranjan Sahu, Medicine
10. Gurcharan Singh, Sports
11. Laxman Singh, Social Work
12. Thounaojam Chaoba Singh, Public Affairs
13. Raveena Tandon, Art

14. Rakesh Radheshyam Jhunjhunwala, Trade & Industry
15. Sudha Murthy, Social Work

Padma Shri 2022 winners: Unsung heroes

1. Rutger Kortenhorst, Literature and Education
2. P Narayana Kurup, Literature and Education
3. K V Rabiya, Social Work
4. Sonu Nigam, Art
5. Avani Lekhara, Sports
6. Dr Narendra Prasad Misra, Medicine
7. Guru Tulku Rinpoche, Spiritualism
8. Brahmanand Sankhwalkar, Sports
9. Anil K. Rajvanshi, Science and Engineering
10. Amai Mahalinga Naik, Agriculture
11. Ryuko Hira, Trade and Industry
12. Avadh Kishore Jadia, Literature and Education
13. Neeraj Chopra, Sports

Padma Shri 2021 winners: Unsung heroes

1. Chandrakant Mehta, Literature and Education
2. Dr. Rattan Lal Mittal, Medicine
3. Madhavan Nambiar, Sports
4. Shyam Sunder Paliwal, Social Work
5. Dr. J N Pande, Medicine
6. Girish Prabhune, Social Work
7. Nanda Prusty, Literature and Education
8. Kanaka Raju, Art
9. Sosamma Iype, Animal Husbandry

Padma Shri 2020 winners: Unsung heroes

1. Shashadhar Acharya, Arts
2. Yogi Aereon, Medicine
3. Jai Prakash Agarwal, Trade & Industry
4. Jagdish Lal Ahuja, Social Work

5. Kazi Masum Akhtar, Literature & Education
6. Khan Zaheerkhan, Sports
7. Raman Gangakhedkar, Science & Engineering
8. Barry Gardiner, Public Affairs
9. Bharat Goenka, Trade & Industry
10. Shanti Jain, Arts
11. Ekta Kapoor, Arts
12. Karan Johar, Arts
13. S. P. Kothari, Literature & Education
14. Prasanta Pattanaik, Literature & Education
15. Tetsu Nakamura, Social Work
16. Jitu Rai, Sports
17. Shanti Roy, Medicine

PARAM VIR CHAKRA RECIPIENTS

Number	Name	Regiment	Date	Place	Notes
IC-521	Major Som Nath Sharma	4th Battalion, Kumaon Regiment	3-Nov-47	Badgam, Kashmir	Posthumous
IC-22356	Lance Naik Karam Singh	1st Battalion, Sikh Regiment	13-Oct-48	Tithwal, Kashmir	
SS-14246	Second Lieutenant Rama Raghoba Rane	Corps of Engineers	8-Apr-48	Naushera, Kashmir	
27373	Naik Jadu Nath Singh	1st Battalion, Rajput Regiment	Feb-48	Naushera, Kashmir	Posthumous
2831592	Company Havildar Major Piru Singh Shekhawat	6th Battalion, Rajputana Rifles	17 July1948– 18July 1948	Tithwal, Kashmir	Posthumous
IC-8497	Captain Gurbachan Singh Salaria	3rd Battalion, 1st Gorkha Rifles (The Malaun Regiment)	5-Dec-61	Elizabethville, Katanga, Congo	Posthumous
IC-7990	Major Dhan Singh Thapa	1st Battalion, 8th Gorkha Rifles	20-Oct-62	Ladakh, India	
JC-4547	Subedar Joginder Singh	1st Battalion, Sikh Regiment	23-Oct-62	Tongpen La, Northeast Frontier Agency, India	Posthumous

IC-7990	Major Shaitan Singh	13th Battalion, Kumaon Regiment	18-Nov-62	Rezang La	Posthumous
2639885	Company Quarter Master Havildar Abdul Hamid	4th Battalion, The Grenadiers	10-Sep-65	Chima, Khem Karan Sector	Posthumous
IC-5565	Lieutenant-Colonel Ardeshir Burzorji Tarapore	17th Poona Horse	15-Oct-65	Phillora, Sialkot Sector, Pakistan	Posthumous
4239746	Lance Naik Albert Ekka	14th Battalion, Brigade of the Guards	3-Dec-71	Gangasagar	Posthumous
10877F(P)	Flying Officer Nirmal Jit Singh Sekhon	No.18 Squadron, Indian Air Force	14-Dec-71	Srinagar, Kashmir	Posthumous
IC-25067	2/Lieutenant Arun Khețarpal	17th Poona Horse	16-Dec-71	Jarpal, Shakargarh Sector	Posthumous
IC-14608	Major Hoshiar Singh	3rd Battalion, The Grenadiers	17-Dec-71	Basantar River, Shakargarh Sector	
JC-155825	Naib Subedar Bana Singh	8th Battalion, Jammu and Kashmir Light Infantry	23- Jun-87	Siachen Glacier, Jammu and Kashmir	
IC-32907	Major Ramaswamy Parameshwaran	8th Battalion, Mahar Regiment	25-Nov-87	Sri Lanka	Posthumous
IC-56959	Captain Manoj Kumar Pandey	1st Battalion, 11th Gorkha Rifles	3-Jul-99	Khaluber/ Juber Top, Batalik sector, Kargil area, J&K	Posthumous
2690572	Grenadier Yogendra Singh Yadav	18th Battalion, The Grenadiers	4-Jul-99	Tiger Hill, Kargil area	
13760533	Rifleman Sanjay Kumar	13th Battalion, Jammu & Kashmir Rifles	5-Jul-99	Area Flat Top, Kargil Area	

IC-57556	Captain Vikram Batra	13th Battalion, Jammu & Kashmir Rifles	6-Jul-99	Point 5140, Point 4875, Kargil Area	Posthumous
13760533	Sub.Major Sanjay Kumar	J&K Rifles	4 July 1999	Kargil War,	Posthumous

INTERNATIONAL GANDHI PEACE PRIZE RECIPIENTS

- Eleanor Roosevelt (1960)
- Edwin T. Dahlberg (1960)
- Rabbi Maurice Eisendrath (1961)
- John Haynes Holmes (1961)
- Linus C. Pauling (1962)
- James Paul Warburg (1962)
- E. Stanley Jones (1963)
- A.J. Muste (1966)
- Norman Thomas (1967)
- Jerome Davis (1967)
- William Sloane Coffin, Jr. (1967)
- Benjamin Spock (1968)
- Wayne Morse (1970)
- Willard Uphaus (1970)
- U Thant (1972)
- Dorothy Day (1975)
- Daniel Ellsberg (1976)
- Peter Benenson and Martin Ennals (1978)
- Roland Bainton (1979)
- Helen Caldicott (1980)
- Corliss Lamont (1981)
- Randall Watson Forsberg (1982)
- Robert Jay Lifton (1984)
- Kay Camp (1984)
- Bernard Lown (1986)
- John Somerville (1987)
- César Chávez (1989)
- Marian Wright Edelman (1990)
- George McGovern (1991)
- Ramsey Clark (1992)
- Lucius Walker, Jr. (1993)
- Roy Bourgeois (1994)
- Edith Ballantyne (1995)
- The New Haven/León Sister City Project (1996)
- Howard and Alice Frazier (1997)
- Michael True (2002)
- Dennis Kucinich (2003)
- Karen Jacob and David Cortright (2004)
- Chandi Prasad Bhatt-India (2023)
- Gita Press---India (2024)

ARJUNA AWARDS

Archery

- 2020 Atanu Das
- 2021 Harvinder Singh
- 2023 Ojas Deotale
- 2024 Rakesh Kumar

Athletics

- 2020 : Dutte Chand
- 2021 : Arpinder Singh
- 2022: Seema Punia, Eldhose Paul, Avinash Sable
- 2023: Murali Sreeshankar, Parul Chaudhary
- 2024: Jyothi Yarraji, Annu Rani, Ajeet Singh Yadav, Preeti Pal, Jeevanji Deepthi, Sachin Sarjerao Khilari, Dharambir Nain, Pranav Soorma, Hokato Hotozhe Sema, Simran Sharma, Navdeep Singh

Badminton

- 2020 : Sat Coiksairaj Rankired
- 2021 : Suhas Yathiraj
- 2022: Lakshya Sen, Prannoy H.S.
- 2024: Manisha Ramadass, Nithya Sre Sivan, Kumar Nitesh, Thulasimathi Murugesan

Boxing

- 2020 : Manish Kaushik, Lovlina Borgohain
- 2021 : Simranjit Kaur
- 2022: Amit Panghal, Nikhat Zareen
- 2023: Mohammad Hussamuddin
- 2024: Saweety Boora, Nitu Ghanghas

Chess

- 2022 : Bhakti Kulkarni
- 2023 : R. Vaishali
- 2024 : Vantika Agarwal

Cricket

- 2020 : Ishant Sharma, Deepti Sharma
- 2021 : Shikhar Dhawan
- 2023: Mohammed Shami, Ajay Kumar Reddy

Equestrian

- 2020 : Saswant A. Anant
- 2023: Anush Agarwalla, Divyakriti Singh

Golf

- 2020 : Aditi Ashok
- 2023: Diksha Dagar

Hockey

- 2020 : Akashdeep Singh
- 2021 : Dilpreet Singh
- 2022: Deep Grace Ekka
- 2023: Krishan Pathak, Sushila Chanu
- 2024: Salima Tete, Abhishek, Sanjay, Jarmanpreet Singh, Sukhjeet Singh

Judo

- 2022: Shushila Devi Likmabam
- 2024: Kapil Parmar

Kabaddi

- 2020 : Deepak Hooda
- 2021 : Sandeep Narwal
- 2022: Sakshi Kumari
- 2023: Pawan Sehrawat, Ritu Negi

Rowing

- 2020 : Dattu Barban Bhokanai

Shooting

- 2020 : Manish Narwal, Manu Bhaker
- 2021 : Abhishek Varma, Singhraj Adhana
- 2022: Elavenil Valarivan, Om Prakash Mitharwal
- 2023: Aishwary Pratap Singh Tomar, Esha Singh
- 2024: Swapnil Kusale, Sarabjot Singh, Rubina Francis, Mona Agarwal

Squash

- 2023: Harinder Pal Sandhu
- 2024: Abhay Singh

Swimming

- 2020 : Suyash Jadhav
- 2022 : Swapnil S. Patil
- 2024 : Sajan Prakash

Table Tennis

- 2020 : Madhurika S. Patkar
- 2021 : Bhavina Patel
- 2022 : Sreeja Akula
- 2023: Ayhika Mukherjee

Wrestling

- 2020 : Divya Kakran
- 2021 : Deepak Purnia
- 2022: Anshu Malik, Sarita Mor
- 2023: Sunil Kumar, Antim Panghal
- 2024: Aman Sehrawat

DADA SAHEB PHALKE AWARDS

Year	Awardee	Occupation
2022	Asha Parekh	Actress
2023	Rekha	Hindi Actress
2024	Mithun Chakraborty	Hindi, Bengali Actor
2025	Mohanlal	Malayalam Actor

NATIONAL HIGHWAYS

N H No.	State Names with Length(km)	Total (Km)
1	Delhi (21.4) Haryana (182.7) Punjab (280.1)	484.2
10	Delhi (20) Haryana (140)	160
11	Rajasthan (260) Uttar Pradesh [24.75]/ Rajasthan [20.25] (90)	350
12	MadhyaPradesh (297) Rajasthan (328)	625
13	Karnataka (194)	194

13,17 and 48	Karnataka (37)	37
14	Gujarat (118.1) Gujarat [34]/Rajasthan [42] (152) Rajasthan (246)	516.1
15	Gujarat (106.2) Punjab (l0l)	207.2
15,8A	Gujarat (90.3)	90.3
17	Goa (139) Kamataka (89) Kerala (451) Maharashtra(84)	763
17B	Goa (13)	13
18	Andhra Pradesh (192.5)	192.5
19,77	Bihar (60)	60
1A	Jammu Kashmir (500.47) Punjab (65.77) Punjab[29]/ Himanchal Pradesh [ll] (80)	646.24
2	Bihar (175) Bihar [10]/Jharkhand [70] (160) Delrii[12]/ Haryana [74]/Uttar Pradesh [113.8] (599.4)Delhi [12]/ Haryana [74] /Uttar Pradesh [59](435) Jharkhand (121.75) Uttar Pradesh (683.49) Uttar Pradesh [55]/ Bihar [21] (152) WestBengal (215.457)	2542.097
2,25	Uttar Pradesh (62.8)	62.8
2,3	Uttar Pradesh (29)	29
200	Chattisgarh (28) Orissa (137)	165
202	AndhraPradesh (30)	30
203	Orissa (59)	59
205	TamilNadu [81.5]/AndhraPradesh [56.5] (276)	276
205,4 and 45	Tamil Nadu (4)	4
21	Punjab (72.9)	72.9
21,22	Haryana [6]/Punjab [30] (72)	72
210	Tamil Nadu (200)	200
215	Orissa (269)	269
22	Haryana [20]/Himachal Pradesh [6.69]/ Punjab [2] (86.07) Himachal Pradesh (l00)	186.07
220	Tamil Nadu (57)	57
24	Uttar Pradesh (463.25)	463.25

25	Madhya Pradesh (35) Madhya Pradesh [30]/ Uttar Pradesh 1] (82) Uttar Pradesh (200.72)	317.72
25, 26	Uttar Pradesh (49.7)	49.7
25,76	Madhya Pradesh (53)	53
26	Madhya Pradesh (275.7) Uttar Pradesh (87.3)	363
27	Uttar Pradesh (6)	6
28	Bihar (159.085) Uttar Pradesh (355.74)	514.825
28A	Bihar (67)	67
3	Madhya Pradesh (221) Maharashtra (375) Rajasthan (20) Uttar Pradesh (16) Uttar Pradesh [7]/Rajasthan [10] (34)	666
30	Bihar (53)	53
31	Assam (164.8) Bihar (298.15) WestBengal (97.85)	560.8
31,31C	WestBengal (201)	201
31C	Assam (93) West Bengal (32)	125
33	Jharkhand (265)	265
34	Jharkhand (0) West Bengal (5.5)	5.5
35	WestBengal (60)	60
36	Assam (154.5)	154.5
37	Assam (142.5)	142.5
39	Manipur (112) Nagaland (28)	140
4	Karnataka (701.124) Maharashtra (387.75) TamilNadu (92.6)	1181.474
4, 45	Tamil Nadu (19)	19
41	WestBengal (53)	53
43	Chattisgarh (23)	23
44	Assam (116) Meghalaya (136) Tripura (195)	447
45	Tamil Nadu (385.273)	385.273
45, 4 and 5	Tamil Nadu (32)	32
45B	Tamil Nadu (252.997)	252.997
45 Ext	Tamil Nadu (73)	73
46	Tamil Nadu (145)	145
47	Kerala (401.6) Tamil Nadu (254.035)	655.635
48	Karnataka (154)	154

49	Tamil Nadu (186)	186
4A	Goa (69) Karnataka (84)	153
4B, 4	Maharashtra (30)	30
5	Andhra Pradesh (1015.77) Orissa (390.398) TamilNadu (41.8)	1447.968
50	Maharashtra (30)	30
52	Assam (314)	314
52A	Arunachal Pradesh (22)Assam (9)	31
54	Assam (353.5) Mizoram (95)	448.5
56A and B	Uttar Pradesh (22.85)	22.85
57	Bihar (299)	299
57A	Bihar (13)	13
58	UttarPradesh (125)	125
58, 72	379 5A Uttar Pradesh[21]/Uttarkhand[56](154)	154
59	Gujarat(210) Madhya Pradesh (169)	379
5A	Orissa(77)	77
6	Chattisgarh (145.685) Gujarat (113) Maharashtra(305.455) Orissa (88) West Bengal (116.582)	768.722
60	Orissa(53.41)WestBkkengal(65.86)	119.27
66	Tamil Nadu (208.61)	208.61
67	Tamil Nadu (209.7)	209.7
67, KC1	Tamil Nadu (59.2)	59.2
67,KC2	Tamil Nadu (55.2)	55.2
67Ex	Tamil Nadu (45)	45
68	Tamil Nadu (136.357)	136.357
69	Madhya Pradesh (13)	13
7	Andhra Pradesh (770.942) Karnataka (184.36)Madhya Pradesh (105.825) Maharashtra (270)Tamil Nadu (687.95)	2019.077
71	Haryana (97)	97
71A	Haryana (73)	73
72	Uttarakhand (69)	69
75	Madhya Pradesh (l00) Madhya Pradesh [68.5]/ Uttar Pradesh [11.5] (160)	260
75,3	Madhya Pradesh (42)	42

76	Rajasthan (654.575)	654.575
76,14	Rajasthan (43)	43
77	Bihar (89)	89
79	Rajasthan (171.87)	171.87
79,76	Rajasthan (30)	30
79A	Rajasthan (36.23)	36.23
7A	Tamil Nadu (47.2)	47.2
8	Delhi (9.7)/Haryana (18) (55.4) Delhi [13] /Haryana [23] (72) Gujarat (583.5) Haryana[55]/Rajasthan[71] (252) Maharashtra (121.4)Rajasthan (418.48)	1502.78
80	Bihar (70)	70
84	Bihar (130)	130
85,19	Bihar (153)	153
86Ex	Madhya Pradesh (40)	40
8A	Gujarat (200.56)	200.56
8B	Gujarat (214)	214
8D	Gujarat (127)	127
9	Andhra Pradesh (324) Maharashtra (170)	494
91	Uttar Pradesh (106)	106
NE1	Gujarat (50)	50
SH54	Maharashtra (14.35)	14.35
SR	Andhra Pradesh (12) Tamil Nadu (30.1)	42.1

RAILWAY ZONES

For administrative purposes, Indian Railways is divided into different zones.

Zone	Abbr.	Headquarters established	Date
Northern Railway	NR	Delhi	April 14, 1952
North Eastern Railway	NER	Gorakhpur	1952
Northeast Frontier Railway	NFR	Maligaon (Guwahati)	1958
Eastern Railway	ER	Kolkata	April, 1952
South Eastern Railway	SER	Kolkata	1955,
South Central Railway	SCR	Secunderabad	October 2,1966

Southern Railway	SR	Chennai	April 14, 1951
Central Railway	CR	Mumbai	November 5, 1951
Western Railway	WR	Mumbai	November 5, 1951
South Western Railway	SWR	Hubli	April 1, 2003
North Western Railway	NWR	Jaipur	Oct 1, 2001
West Central Railway	WCR	Jabalpur	April 1, 2003
North Central Railway	NCR	Allahabad	April 1, 2003
South East Central Railway	SECR	Bilaspur, CG	April 1, 2003
East Central Railway	ECoR	Bhubaneswar	April 1, 2003
Railway East Coast	ECR	Hajipur	Oct 1, 2002
Konkan Railway	KR	Navi Mumbai	Jan 26,1998

Zonal Railway	Division
Northern Railway	Delhi, Ambala, Firozpur, Lucknow, Moradabad
North Eastern Railway	Izzatilagar, Lucknow, Varanasi
Zonal Railway	Division
Northeast Frontier Railway	Alipurduar, Katihar, Lumding, Rangia, Tinsukia
Eastern Railway	Howrah, Sealdah, Asansol, Malda
South Eastern Railway	Adra, Chakradharpur, Kharagpur, Ranchi
South Central Railway	Secunderabad, Hyderabad, Guntakal, Guntur, Nanded, Vijayawada
Southern Railway	Chennai, Madurai, Palghat, Tiruchchirapalli, Trivandrum, Salem
Central Railway	Mumbai, Bhusawal, Pune, Solapur, Nagpur
Western Railway	Mumbai Central, Baroda, Ratlam, Ahmedabad, Rajkot, Bhavnagar
South Western Railway	Hubli, Bangalore, Mysore
North Western Railway	Jaipur, Ajmer, Bikaner, Jodhpur
West Central Railway	Jabalpur, Bhopal, Kota
North Central Railway	Allahabad, Agra, Jhansi
South East Central Railway	Bilaspur, Raipur, Nagpur
East Coast Railway	Khurda Road, Sambalpur, Visakhapatnam
East Central Railway	Danapur, Dhanbad, Mughalsarai, Samastipur, Sonpur

LIST OF FAST TRAINS

Sr. No.	Train number (outbound/ inbound)	Train name	Origin	Destination	Round trip distance (km)	Round trip time (h:m)	Commercial speed km/h
1	12001/12002	Bhopal Shatabdi[3]	Bhopal Junction	New Delhi	1402 km	15:40	91.03 km/h
2	12033/12034	Kanpur Reverse Shatabdi	Kanpur Central	New Delhi	874 km	9:55	88.13 km/h
3	12275/12276	Allahaba d Duronto	Allahabad	New Delhi	1268 km	14:45	87.75 km/h
4	12951/12952	Mumbai Rajdhani	Mumbai Central	New Delhi	2768 km	31:55:00	86.7 km/h [4]
5	12301/12302	Howrah Rajdhani	Howrah (Kolkata)	New Delhi	2894 km	33:55:00	85.33 km/h
6	12273/12274	Howrah Duronto	Howrah (Kolkata)	New Delhi	2887 km	34:05:00	83.92 km/h
7	12313/12314	Sealdah Rajdhani Express	Sealdah (Kolkata)	New Delhi	2908 km	35:10:00	82.69 km/h
8	12909/12910	Bandra Terminus Garib Rath	Bandra Terminus (Mumbai)	Hazrat Nizamuddin (Delhi)	2732 km	33:30:00	81.55 km/h
9	12249/12250	Howrah-New Delhi Yuva Express	Howrah	New Delhi	2894 km	35:83	80.77 km/h
10	12003/12004	Lucknow Swarna Shatabdi	Lucknow	New Delhi	1022 km	12:45	80.16 km/h
11	12281/12282	Bhubaneshwar Duranto	Bhubaneshwar	New Delhi	3492 km	43.55	79.51 km/h
12	12953/12954	August Kranti Rajdhani	Mumbai Central	Hazrat Nizamuddin (Delhi)	2754 km	34:40:00	79.44 km/h
13	12247/12248	Bandra Terminus-H. Nizamuddin Yuva Express	Bandra Terminus	Hazrat Nizamuddin (Delhi)	2732 km	34:40:00	78.8 km/h
14	12309/12310	Patna Rajdhani Express	Rajendra Nagar (Patna)	New Delhi	2002 km	25:25:00	78.77 km/h
15	12269/12270	Chennai Duronto	Chennai Central	Hazrat Nizamuddin (Delhi)	4352 km	56:15:00	77.37 km/h
16	12433/12434	Chennai Rajdhani	Chennai Central	Hazrat Nizamuddin (Delhi)	4352 km	56:25:00	77.14 km/h
17	12611/12612	Chennai Garib Rath	Chennai Central	Hazrat Nizamuddin (Delhi)	4352 km	56:25:00	77.15 km/h

18	12285/12286	Secunderabad Duronto		Hazrat Nizamuddin (Delhi)	3320 km	43.15	76.76 km/h
19	12439/12440	Ranchi Rajdhani	Ranchi	New Delhi	2612 km	34:10:00	76.45 km/h
20	12437/12438	Secunderabad Rajdhani	Secunderabad Railway Station (Hyderabad)	Hazrat Nizamuddin (Delhi)	3320 km	43:35:00	76.18 km/h
21	12421/12422	Bhubaneshwar Rajdhani	Bhubaneshwar	New Delhi	3448 km	45:45:00	75.37 km/h
22	12263/12264	Pune Duronto	Pune	Hazrat Nizamuddin (Delhi)	3028 km	40:20:00	75.07 km/h
23	12005/12006	Kalka Shatabdi	Kalka	New Delhi	606 km	8.5	74.96 km/h
24	12261/12262	Mumbai -Howrah Duronto	Chhatrapati Shivaji Terminus (Mumbai)	Howrah (Kolkata)	3936 km	52:35km/h	74.85
25	12877/12878	Ranchi Garib Rath	Ranchi	New Delhi	2685 km	36:10:00	74.24 km/h
26	12267/12268	Ahmedabad Duranto	Ahmedabad	Mumbai (Mumbai Central)	982 km	13.2	73.65 km/h
27	12029/12030	Swarna Shatabdi	New Delhi	Amritsar	896 km	12:10	73.64 km/h
28	12013/12014	Amritsar Shatabdi	New Delhi	Amritsar	896 km	12:10	73.64 km/h
29	12441/12442	Bilaspur Rajdhani	New Delhi	Bilaspur	3002 km	41	73.22 km/h
30	12289/12290	Mumbai -Nagpur Duronto	Chhatrapati Shivaji Terminus (Mumbai)	Nagpur	1674 km	23:00	72.78 km/h
31	12353/12354	Rajendra Nagar Garib Rath	Rajendra Nagar (Patna)	Hazrat Nizamuddin (Delhi)	1996 km	27:30:00	72.58 km/h
32	12027/12028	Bangalore Shatabdi	Chennai Central	Bangalore City	724 km	10:00	72.40 km/h
33	12155/12156	Shaan - E - Bhopal Express	Bhopal Habibganj, Bhopal	Hazrat Nizamuddin, Delhi	1408 km	15:35	72.19 km/h
34	12061/12062	Bhopal Jan Shatabdi	Bhopal	Jabalpur Junction	916 km	12:50	71.38 km/h
35	12009/12010	Ahmedabad Shatabdi	Mumbai	Ahmedabad	982 km	13:50	70.99 km/h
36	12429/12430	Bangalore Rajdhani Express	Bangalore City	New Delhi	4764 km	67:20:00	70.75 km/h
37	12007/12008	Mysore Shatabdi	Chennai Central	Mysore	1000 km	14:10	70.59 km/h
38	12451/12452	Shram Shakti Express	Kanpur Central	New Delhi	880 km	12:30	70.40 km/h
39	22435/22436	Vande Bharat	Kanpur Central	New Delhi	880 km	12:30	70.40 km/h

COMMERCIAL AIRLINES INTERNATIONAL ROUTES

Air India	Air India Express
Asia India	Indian Airlines
Jet Airways	Go Air
Vistara	Spice Jet

DOMESTIC AIRLINES IN INDIA

Indian Airlines

Indian Airlines is India's government owned, full service domestic airline, based in Mumbai. The airline was merged with Air India, the government owned international airline, in 2007 but still retains its name. Its market share has dropped significantly, to around 14%, in recent years.

Jet Airways

Jet Airways is widely regarded as India's biggest and best airline. It's a privately owned, full service airline that commenced operating in mid 1993. It's now captured almost 23% of the market, and has bases in Delhi, Mumbai, Pune, Kolkata, Hyderabad, Chennai, and Bangalore. Jet Airways has won many awards for quality service.

Vistara

Tata SIA Airlines Limited, operating as Vistara, is an Indian domestic airline based in Gurgaon with its hub at Delhi-Indira Gandhi International Airport. The airline had carried more than two million passengers by June 2016 and as of April 2016, has a 2.3% share of the domestic carrier market. The airline operates to seventeen destinations with a fleet of Airbus A320-200 aircraft. Vistara was the first airline to introduce premium economy seats on domestic routes in India.

IndiGo Airlines

Indigo Airlines is based in Delhi and flies to around 15 destinations all over India. This privately owned airline started operating in mid-2006, and has a market share of almost 11%. It's considered to be India's best low cost carrier. Its airplanes are new and clean, and despite keeping fares low, the airline hasn't compromised on punctuality, connectivity of flights, safety, or customer service.

SpiceJet

SpiceJet is another decent, privately owned, low cost carrier. The airline, which is based in Delhi, started operating in mid- 2005. It has just over 10% share of the market, and services most capital cities in India.

Go Air

Go Air is a small privately owned, low cost airline that started operating in late 2005. It has almost a 5% market share and operates a fleet of brightly colored airplanes to twelve cities in India. Its remote destinations include Jammu, Srinagar, and Guwahati.

Paramount Airways

Paramount Airways is a small, privately owned airline based in Madurai in south India. It started operating in late October 2005, and has a 1.5% market share. The airline flies to nine destinations in south India, with its main hub in Chennai. The average age of its airplanes is three and a half years.

Air Asia

India is an Indian low cost carrier headquartered in Chennai, India. The airline is a joint venture with Air Asia Berhad holding 49% stake in the airline,

Tata Sons holding 40.06% and Arun Bhatia holding the remaining 10% through his company, Telestra Tradeplace. Air Asia India commenced operations on 12 June 2014 with Bangalore as its primary hub.

FIVE YEAR PLANS OF INDIA

- First Five-Year Plan, 1951–1956
- Second Five-Year Plan, 1956–1961
- Third Five-Year Plan, 1961–1966
- Fourth Five-Year Plan, 1969–1974
- Fifth Five-Year Plan, 1974–1979
- Sixth Five-Year Plan, 1980–1985
- Seventh Five-Year Plan, 1985–1990
- Period between 1989–1991
- Eighth Five-Year Plan, 1992–1997
- Ninth Five Year Plan, 1997–2002
- Tenth Five-Year Plan, 2002–2007
- Eleventh Five-Year Plan, 2007–2012
- Twelth Five Year Plan,2012--2017
- Thirteenth Five Year Plan, ,2017--2022
- Fourteenth Five Year Plan ,2022-2027

INDIAN SPACE RESEARCH ORGANISATION

The Indian Space Research Organisation is the primary body for space research under the control of the Government of India, and one of the leadingspaceresearchorganizationsintheworld. Itwasestablishedinits modern form in 1969 as a result of coordinated efforts initiated earlier. Taking into consideration its budget, it is among the most efficient space organizations on the globe. Over the years, ISRO has conducted a variety of operations for both Indian and foreign clients. ISRO's satellite launch capability is mostly provided by indigenous launch vehicles and launch sites. In 2008, ISRO successfully launched its first lunar probe, Chandrayaan-1, while future plans include indigenous development of GSLV, manned space missions, further lunar exploration, and interplanetary probes.

Established	August 15, 1969 (41 years ago)
Headquarters	Antariksh Bhavan, New BEL Road, Bangalore, India

Primary spaceport Satish Dhawan Space Centre
Administrator A. S. Kiran Kumar (Chairman)
Budget 79.27 billion INR (2015-16)

Satellite	Launch Date	Launch Vehicle	Type of Satellite
CMS 01	17 Dec 2020	PSLV-C50	Communication satellite
INSAT 3DS	17 Feb 2024	GSLV-F14 / INSAT-3DS	Mission Climate & environment satellite
EOS 08	16 Aug 2024	SSLV-D3 / EOS-08	Mission Earth observation satellite
GSAT N2	19 Nov 2024	Falcon-9 / GSAT-20 (GSAT-N2)	Communication satellite
NVS 02	29 Jan 2025	GSLV-F15 / NVS-02	Mission Navigation satellite (NavIC system)
EOS 09	18 May 2025	PSLV-C61 / EOS-09	Mission Earth-observation radar imaging satellite
PSLV -C61/EoS--09	18-5-2025		Navigation Satellite
Axiom	4--5 June 2025		
NISAR	30 Jul 2025	GSLV-F16 / NISAR	Mission Joint Earth-observation radar satellite (ISRO-NASA)

MONUMENTAL HERITAGE OF INDIA

India's Famous Monuments

India is an ancient country rich in monumental heritage which are the speaking stones of India's authentic architectural and historical details.

Tombs and Mosques

- Taj Mahal, Agra
- Humayun Tomb, Delhi
- Jama Masjid, Delhi
- Qutub Minar, Delhi

Caves

- Ajanta Caves, Aurangabad
- Elephanta Caves, Mumbai
- Ellora Caves, Aurangabad

- Udaygiri Caves, Bhubaneshwar
- Kandhagiri Caves, Bhubaneshwar
- Edakkal Caves, Kerala
- Borra Caves, Vishakapatnam

Doors and Gates

- Buland Darwaza, Fatehpur Sikri
- Charminar, Hyderabad
- Gateway of India, Mumbai
- India Gate, Delhi

Forts and Palaces

- Old Fort, Delhi
- Red Fort, Delhi
- Red Fort, Agra
- City Palace, Jaipur
- City Palace, Udaipur
- Golconda Fort, Hyderabad
- Havelis of Delhi
- Havelis of Shekhawati, Rajasthan
- Hawa Mahal, Jaipur
- Jaisalmer Havelis
- Jal Mahal, Jaipur
- Mysore Palace
- Bidar Fort, Karnataka
- Gingee Fort, Tamil Nadu

Heritage Palaces

- Ajit Bhawan Palace
- Bhanwar Niwas Palace
- Gorbandh Palace
- Castle Mandawa
- Khimsar Fort
- Mansingh Palace Hotel
- Samode Palace
- Jai Mahal Palace
- Jai Vilas Palace
- Lake Palace
- Lalgarh Palace
- Narayan Niwas Palace, Jaisalmer
- Rang Mahal Palace,Jaisalmer
- Sariska Palace
- Shiv Niwas Palace
- Umaid Bhawan Palace

Temples

- Khajuraho Temples
- Jagannath Puri Temple
- Konark Sun Temple
- Meenakshi Temple
- Tirupati Balaji Temple
- Brihadisvara Temple

- Omkareshwar Temple
- Dwarka Temple
- Golden Temple
- Akshardham Temple
- Mahabalipuram Temples
- Ram Mandir, Ayodhya
- Swaminarayan Akshardham (Delhi)
- Birla Radha Krishna Mandir, Goa
- Sri Lakshmi Narasimha Swamy Temple, Yadadri
- Murugan Temple, Kodungaiyur
- Kashi Vishwanath Corridor, Varanasi

Religious Monuments

- Sanchi Stupa
- Monuments of Hampi
- Bangla Sahib Gurudwara, Delhi
- Nalanda University
- Monuments of Bodh Gaya
- Lotus Temple, Delhi

Some other Famous Monuments

- Jantar Mantar, Delhi
- Qutub Minar, Delhi

❑❑❑

Current Affairs from 2020-26

11

EVENT IN 2020

January 2020

1. 03/01/2020: A U.S. drone strike near Baghdad Airport killed Iranian General Qassem Soleimani, sharply escalating US–Iran tensions.
2. 07/01/2020: Chinese authorities and researchers identified a novel coronavirus (later named SARS-CoV-2) as the cause of pneumonia clusters in Wuhan.
3. 20/01/2020: The first confirmed COVID-19 case in the United States was publicly recognized, beginning heightened US public-health focus.
4. 23/01/2020: Wuhan and several Chinese cities instituted lockdowns and travel restrictions to contain the virus outbreak.
5. 25/01/2020: India confirmed its first COVID-19 case (Kerala), marking the official arrival of the virus in the country.
6. 31/01/2020: The United Kingdom formally left the European Union's political institutions, starting the transition period (Brexit).

February 2020

1. 02/02/2020: China began large-scale efforts to treat and contain COVID-19 as cases rose beyond Wuhan and Hubei province.
2. 21/02/2020: Italy reported a major outbreak in Lombardy and other northern regions, becoming Europe's early COVID-19 hotspot.
3. 24/02/2020: Iran acknowledged a growing COVID-19 outbreak with clusters and several deaths, raising regional alarm.
4. 29/02/2020: The WHO continued to monitor international spread as cases appeared across multiple continents.
5. February 2020 (throughout): Global supply-chain disruptions began as Chinese factory slowdowns affected manufacturing and trade.

6. February 2020 (US politics): The U.S. Democratic primary campaign intensified as candidates competed for delegates.

March 2020

1. 11/03/2020: WHO declared COVID-19 a global pandemic, prompting urgent national responses worldwide.
2. 13/03/2020: Governments across Europe and North America began closing borders, banning large gatherings and restricting travel.
3. 24/03/2020: India announced a nationwide lockdown to combat COVID-19, affecting 1.3 billion people.
4. 03/2020 (early): Global stock markets plunged and central banks announced emergency monetary measures.
5. 2020 Mar (sports): Tokyo 2020 Olympics were effectively postponed as organizers and IOC faced health risks (official postponement announced soon after).

April 2020

1. April 2020 (healthcare): ICUs in hotspot regions faced severe strain and health systems scrambled for beds and staff.
2. 2020 Apr: Worldwide emissions and some pollution levels temporarily declined due to reduced transport and industrial activity.
3. April 2020 (economy): Unemployment claims surged in multiple economies; governments expanded emergency welfare support.
4. April 2020 (education): Schools and universities shifted to online learning, exposing digital-divide challenges.

May 2020

1. 25/05/2020: George Floyd was killed in Minneapolis, triggering global Black Lives Matter protests against racial injustice.
2. May 2020 (reopening): Many countries began phased "reopening" plans while monitoring infection resurgence risks.
3. May 2020 (economy): Economists revised global GDP forecasts downward as prolonged restrictions damaged demand.
4. May 2020 (technology): Remote-work tools and e-commerce adoption surged as consumers and firms adjusted.
5. May 2020 (India): Lockdown relaxations were implemented in phases with localized containment strategies.

June 2020

1. 01/06/2020 (US): Many U.S. cities continued protests and policy debates over policing reform after George Floyd's death.
2. June 2020 (economy): Governments weighed extended stimulus measures as unemployment remained high.
3. June 2020 (education): Debates intensified over school reopenings, safety protocols and learning loss mitigation.
4. June 2020 (India/China): Border tensions between India and China in Ladakh escalated after clashes in June.

July 2020

1. 07/2020 (pandemic): Many countries saw periodic surges and localized lockdowns amid reopening.
2. 07/2020 (economic): Central banks and treasuries continued support packages; focus shifted to long-term recovery plans.
3. 07/2020 (US politics): The U.S. presidential campaign adapted to pandemic realities with virtual events and altered strategies.
4. 07/2020 (technology): Telehealth and digital services continued rapid expansion under social-distancing norms.

August 2020

1. 04/08/2020: A massive explosion at Beirut port caused widespread destruction, killing hundreds and deepening Lebanon's crisis.
2. 08/2020 (US politics): Political debates continued over economic relief packages and pandemic response ahead of the U.S. election.
3. 08/2020 (tech): Antitrust and content-moderation debates escalated around major social-media platforms.
4. 08/2020 (India): India reported rising COVID-19 cases and managed localized healthcare surges across states.
5. August 2020 (education): Policymakers planned hybrid and remote models for upcoming school years amid public-health uncertainty.

September 2020

1. 01/09/2020: The global focus remained on vaccine approvals, safety data and production planning for distribution.
2. 15/09/2020 (India): India and China continued diplomatic talks after the June border clashes while troops remained in forward positions.

3. 09/2020 (US): Supreme Court appointments and legal battles shaped political discourse ahead of the election.
4. 09/2020 (economy): Fiscal deficits and sovereign debt sustainability emerged as medium-term policy concerns.
5. 09/2020 (climate): Preparations for major climate summits and renewed commitments were discussed despite pandemic limits.

October 2020

1. 02/10/2020: Global COVID case counts continued to climb as northern-hemisphere countries entered autumn/winter season.
2. 05/10/2020 (India): Ongoing farmer protests intensified in parts of India over new agricultural laws (peaking through late 2020).
3. 10/2020 (US election): The U.S. presidential race between Donald Trump and Joe Biden reached a decisive phase with debates and campaigning.
4. 10/2020 (science): Several vaccine candidates reported interim phase-3 efficacy results, fueling optimism and supply planning.

November 2020

1. 03/11/2020: The U.S. presidential election was held; vote counting followed and controversies over mail ballots emerged.
2. 07/11/2020: Major vaccine developers (e.g., Pfizer/BioNTech) announced strong interim efficacy results, starting distribution planning.
3. 11/2020 (global): Many countries prepared winter contingency plans to manage healthcare loads and vaccination logistics.
4. 11/2020 (India): Protests by farmers around Delhi continued, maintaining national focus on agricultural policy.

December 2020

1. 08/12/2020: The UK began its national COVID vaccination programme using Pfizer/BioNTech doses, a landmark step in mass immunization.
2. 14/12/2020: The United States started administering COVID-19 vaccines (Pfizer) under EUA, initiating a phased rollout.
3. 12/2020 (global): New SARS-CoV-2 variants were detected (e.g., UK variant), raising concerns about transmissibility.
4. 12/2020 (economy): Governments debated further stimulus as parts of Europe and the US entered renewed restrictions.
5. 25/12/2020: Throughout the holiday season, countries warned against travel and large gatherings amid second-wave surges.

EVENT IN 2021

January 2021

1. 06/01/2021: A mob stormed the U.S. Capitol in Washington, D.C., disrupting the certification of the 2020 presidential election and prompting national security concerns.
2. 20/01/2021: Joe Biden was inaugurated as the 46th President of the United States, marking a major transition in U.S. policy and tone.
3. 01/01–Jan 2021: Global COVID vaccination campaigns ramped up while countries struggled with supply and prioritization.
4. 26/01/2021 (India): Farmer protests culminated in clashes and a controversial tractor rally in Delhi on Republic Day, drawing massive attention.

February 2021

1. 01/02/2021 (Myanmar): Myanmar's military carried out a coup d'état on 1 February, detaining leaders and prompting nationwide protests.
2. 13/02/2021: The U.S. and other countries ramped sanctions and diplomatic responses to address geopolitical flashpoints and human-rights concerns.
3. Feb 2021 (India): India continued its vaccine drive with emergency-use approvals for additional vaccines and manufacturing scale-up.
4. 15/02/2021 (space): Space missions and private-sector launches (e.g., commercial crew and reusable rockets) continued to grow in 2021.
5. Feb 2021 (economy): Global markets began pricing in a post-pandemic recovery, but uneven vaccination created divergence across regions.

March 2021

1. 11/03/2021: One year after WHO's pandemic declaration, many countries marked anniversaries while vaccination scaled up unevenly worldwide.
2. 01–03/2021 (India): India's vaccination drive accelerated with expanded eligibility and domestic production ramping up.
3. 03/2021 (US): The U.S. Congress passed further COVID relief and stimulus measures to support households and businesses.
4. 03/2021 (India): Farmer unions continued negotiations and protests while political dialogue carried on intermittently.

April 2021

1. 01/04/2021 (India): India began to see a dramatic surge in COVID-19 cases, signalling the start of a devastating second wave.
2. 07/04/2021: Global concern rose as hospital systems in India became overwhelmed and oxygen shortages emerged.
3. April 2021 (global): Vaccine inequity debates intensified as richer countries secured the majority of early doses.
4. 04/2021 (economy): Supply-chain bottlenecks reappeared with reopening demand and pandemic disruptions.

May 2021

1. 05/2021 (India): India peaked in daily COVID cases in mid-May, reporting record daily infections and deaths in many states.
2. 16/05/2021 (global): Several nations donated vaccines and medical supplies to India while ramping up diplomatic coordination.
3. May 2021 (finance): Markets reacted to reopening prospects and inflationary signals as economies resumed activity.
4. May 2021 (Middle East): May saw renewed hostilities between Israel and Hamas, resulting in significant casualties and international concern.

June 2021

1. 01/06/2021: G7 and other high-level meetings emphasized vaccine sharing, infrastructure investment and economic recovery plans.
2. 11–13/06/2021 (EU/US): Major summits addressed trade, climate and technology competition with China and Russia.
3. June 2021 (India): Vaccination eligibility broadened and domestic manufacturing increased to meet national demand.
4. June 2021 (economy): Inflation warnings emerged in some economies as recovery spending rose.
5. June 2021 (environment): Extreme-weather events underscored urgency for climate adaptation planning.

July 2021

1. 23/07/2021: The Tokyo Olympics (postponed from 2020) opened under strict COVID precautions and limited spectator attendance.
2. 07/2021 (India): Continued vaccination rollouts and local restrictions aimed at controlling outbreaks in various states.

3. July 2021 (economy): Central banks monitored inflation signals while emphasizing that many economies remained below pre-pandemic output.
4. 07/2021 (climate): Heatwaves and floods in multiple regions reinforced climate-risk discussions at policymaker levels.
5. 31/07/2021: Global debates about booster shots versus first-dose coverage in low-income countries intensified.
6. July 2021 (technology): Cybersecurity incidents and ransomware attacks increased, targeting infrastructure and corporations.

August 2021

1. 15/08/2021: The Taliban entered Kabul and took control of Afghanistan as U.S. and NATO forces completed withdrawal, triggering evacuations.
2. 26/08/2021: A terrorist bombing at Kabul airport during evacuation killed many Afghans and foreign service personnel, worsening the crisis.
3. 08/2021 (India): India continued vaccination expansion and grappled with variants and local containment strategies.
4. Aug 2021 (climate): Severe floods and extreme events worldwide highlighted adaptation gaps and humanitarian needs.
5. 31/08/2021: International debates continued on handling refugees, recognising Taliban governance and humanitarian access.
6. August 2021 (economy): Global supply disruptions and shipping logjams affected trade and inventories across industries.

September 2021

1. 01/09/2021: Global vaccine campaigns progressed but unevenly; many low-income countries still awaited broad access.
2. September 2021 (climate): Preparations and commitments ramped up ahead of COP26 with renewed pledges from several nations.
3. Sept 2021 (India): The government expanded digital health credentials and vaccination certificates for travel and access.
4. 09/2021 (politics): Several countries faced political transitions, elections or major government reshuffles.
5. 30/09/2021: Economic recovery narratives were tempered by concerns over debt, inequality and persistent unemployment.
6. Sept 2021 (tech): Regulatory scrutiny of big technology platforms increased in the US, EU and Asia.

October 2021

1. 04/10/2021: The global COVID-19 death toll reached staggering totals; vaccination and treatment remained priorities.
2. 10/2021 (COP26 prep): Countries finalized pre-COP pledges and targets, with intense diplomacy ahead of the summit.
3. Oct 2021 (economy): Supply constraints and energy prices began to feed through into higher consumer prices in many countries.
4. Oct 2021 (India): Economic activity picked up with festivals and domestic demand, though recovery remained uneven.
5. 31/10/2021: Technology policy and privacy regulation debates continued as digital platforms expanded influence.
6. October 2021 (social): Movements for social justice and labour rights persisted in multiple regions, reflecting post-pandemic shifts.

November 2021

1. 01/11/2021: World leaders gathered for COP26 in Glasgow later in the month to negotiate climate actions and finance.
2. 08/11/2021 (global): Discussions at multilateral forums focused on vaccine access, economic recovery and climate finance.
3. 11/11/2021: COP26 (end-Nov) saw major pledges on methane, coal and finance but delegates debated sufficiency and timelines.
4. Nov 2021 (India): India engaged in global climate diplomacy while managing domestic economic reopening.
5. Nov 2021 (economy): Energy prices and supply constraints created near-term inflationary pressures in Europe and Asia.
6. 30/11/2021: The Omicron variant was identified in late November, immediately raising global alarm and travel restrictions.

December 2021

1. 01/12/2021: Omicron (B.1.1.529) variant reports led many countries to reimpose travel limits and accelerate booster campaigns.
2. 10/12/2021 (global): Governments scrambled to update public-health guidance and vaccination strategies in response to Omicron.
3. 12/2021 (economy): Central banks and policy makers began planning responses to persistent inflation signals into 2022.
4. 15/12/2021 (India): India monitored Omicron cases and adjusted testing and border protocols while expanding booster eligibility debates.

5. 31/12/2021: Year-end summaries emphasized that pandemic management, vaccine equity and climate action remained top global priorities.

EVENT IN 2022

January 2022

1. 1 Jan – India begins UNSC Presidency rotation. India assumed the rotating presidency of the United Nations Security Council for January.
2. 6 Jan – U.S. marks first anniversary of Capitol Hill attack. Vigils and political debates highlighted democratic challenges.
3. 10 Jan – Novak Djokovic denied entry into Australia. His visa was cancelled due to COVID-19 vaccination status before the Australian Open.
4. 15 Jan – Massive volcanic eruption near Tonga. The Hunga Tonga–Hunga Ha apai volcano caused tsunamis and atmospheric shockwaves worldwide.
5. 17 Jan – Microsoft acquires Activision Blizzard. In a landmark $69 billion deal, Microsoft expanded its gaming empire.
6. 23 Jan – Burkina Faso military coup. The army ousted President Roch Marc Kaboré, citing insecurity from Islamist insurgency.

February 2022

1. 4 Feb – Beijing Winter Olympics open. Games faced diplomatic boycotts and strict COVID protocols.
2. 6 Feb – Queen Elizabeth II marks Platinum Jubilee. She completed 70 years on the throne, becoming the UK's longest-reigning monarch.
3. 14 Feb – Russia–Ukraine tensions rise sharply. Russian troops massed at Ukraine's border, sparking invasion fears.
4. 15 Feb – India bans over 50 Chinese apps. The move cited data security concerns amid geopolitical tensions.
5. 20 Feb – IPL Mega Auction 2022 concludes. Several players fetched record prices, shaping the cricket season.

March 2022

1. 4 Mar – Russian troops seize Zaporizhzhia nuclear plant. Fears of a nuclear disaster spread worldwide.

2. 7 Mar – South Korea elects Yoon Suk-yeol as President. He defeated Lee Jae-myung in a tight contest.
3. 10 Mar – Assembly elections in India. BJP retained power in Uttar Pradesh, Uttarakhand, Goa, and Manipur; AAP won Punjab.
4. 11 Mar – WHO confirms 6 million COVID deaths worldwide. The grim milestone reflected global health challenges.
5. 16 Mar – Pakistan PM Imran Khan faces no-confidence motion. Political crisis deepened amid opposition moves.
6. 18 Mar – India's INS Shivaji awarded President's Colour. The naval engineering training establishment received the highest honor.

April 2022

1. 3 Apr – Hungary re-elects Viktor Orbán. He secured a fourth consecutive term despite EU criticism.
2. 10 Apr – Imran Khan loses no-confidence vote. Shehbaz Sharif became the new Prime Minister of Pakistan.
3. 13 Apr – Indian Prime Minister inaugurates Pradhanmantri Sangrahalaya. The museum honors contributions of all Indian PMs.
4. 18 Apr – Elon Musk offers to buy Twitter for $44 billion. The deal triggered global debate about free speech and social media.
5. 21 Apr – Russia halts gas supplies to Poland and Bulgaria. Energy became a weapon amid the Ukraine war.
6. 24 Apr – Emmanuel Macron re-elected President of France. He defeated far-right challenger Marine Le Pen.

May 2022

1. 02/05/2022: A draft U.S. Supreme Court opinion to overturn *Roe v. Wade* was leaked, sparking national protests and debate.
2. 14/05/2022: A mass shooting at a supermarket in Buffalo, New York killed 10 people, highlighting ongoing concerns about gun violence in the U.S.
3. 16/05/2022: Karine Jean-Pierre becomes first Black woman and first openly LGBTQ person to serve as U.S. Press Secretary.
4. 17/05/2022: The United States records its 1 millionth death due to COVID-19.
5. 18/05/2022: Finland and Sweden formally begin the process to join NATO, following security concerns arising from the Russia-Ukraine war.

June 2022

1. 24/06/2022: The U.S. Supreme Court overturns *Roe v. Wade*, eliminating federal constitutional protection for abortion rights.
2. 26-28/06/2022: The 48th G7 Summit takes place in Germany, focusing on global economic recovery, climate, and managing the fallout from Russia's invasion.
3. June 2022 (ongoing): Inflation surges in many parts of the world, with prices rising steeply for energy, food, housing, leading to cost-of-living crises.
4. June 2022: Global COVID-19 vaccination continues, but issues of equity and new variants (like Omicron subvariants) remain pressing.
5. June 2022 (US domestic): The U.S. House Select Committee begins hearings into the 6 January 2021 Capitol attack.

July 2022

1. July 2022: Severe heatwaves continue globally; many records broken for hottest temperatures, especially in Europe and the US.
2. July 2022 (Ukraine war): Fighting continues, especially in eastern Ukraine; Russian missile strikes disrupt civilian infrastructure.
3. July 2022 (economy): Reopening economies face supply chain bottlenecks, inflationary pressures, and energy crises.
4. July 2022 (science): Websites and social media report that the James Webb Space Telescope's first images are released, showing deep space with unprecedented clarity.

August 2022

1. August 2022: Devastating floods occur in Pakistan, affecting millions and resulting in massive damage to homes and infrastructure.
2. Aug 2022 (global): Energy supply shocks worsen as Europe tries to reduce dependence on Russian gas and oil.
3. Aug 2022 (politics): Many governments experience political turbulence or policy reorientation in wake of inflation and economic stress.
4. Late Aug 2022: Continued COVID-19 variant monitoring and booster campaigns in many countries.

September 2022

1. 08/09/2022: Queen Elizabeth II died at Balmoral Castle; her son Charles became King Charles III.

2. 15/09/2022: The UK held mourning and transition ceremonies; global reactions and the Commonwealth's future under new king were discussed.
3. Sep 2022 (Ukraine war): Russian referendums begin in occupied regions of Ukraine, drawing condemnation and sanctions.
4. Sep 2022 (population): On 15 November (but events in September preparing for it) the world reached a population milestone of 8 billion, with demographic concerns rising.

October 2022

1. October 2022: Inflation and energy crises deepen through Europe, with winter preparedness becoming a major concern.
2. Oct 2022 (Ukraine war): Missile strikes by Russia on civilian targets and power grids intensified.

November 2022

1. 15/11/2022: The world officially reached 8 billion people.
2. Nov 2022: Mauna Loa volcano in Hawaii erupted after decades of dormancy, raising alerts near populated areas.
3. Nov 2022 (storms/disasters): Severe storms, landslides, industrial accidents and climate-related disasters impacted several countries.

December 2022

1. 06/12/2022: Powerful earthquakes struck Indonesia (Bali and Java region), causing damage and casualties.
2. 12/12/2022: A major sandstorm hit Beijing and north China, with severe air pollution (PM10 levels exceeding safe limits).
3. 15–27/12/2022: Blizzards and winter storms in US (Buffalo etc.) claimed dozens of lives, disrupted power supply and travel during the holiday season.

EVENT IN 2023

January 2023

1. 1-2 January 2023 – Terror attacks in Dangri village, Rajouri district (J&K): terrorists opened fire and planted an IED, killing 7 people and injuring several others.

2. 3 January 2023 – Prime Minister Narendra Modi inaugurated the 108th Indian Science Congress via video conferencing; event to be held from Jan 3-7 in Nagpur.
3. 8-9 January 2023 – The International Kite Festival 2023 began in Ahmedabad; the Government of UP launched its "UP Global City" campaign.
4. 9 January 2023 – Historic Shahi Masjid in Saidabad (Prayagraj, Uttar Pradesh) was demolished for road-widening.
5. 18 January 2023 – Indian wrestlers, including Vinesh Phogat, Bajrang Punia and others, staged protests at Jantar Mantar, New Delhi, against alleged sexual harassment in Wrestling Federation of India.
6. 19 January 2023 – National Disaster Response Force (NDRF) celebrated its 18th Raising Day.

February 2023

1. 11-15 February 2023 – Amritpex 2023: A national philatelic exhibition held in New Delhi (theme: Azadi Ka Amrit Mahotsav); special stamps/ covers/releases.
2. 28 February 2023 – India Government planned to create ten Clean Plant Centres to enhance fruit crop production.
3. 28 February 2023 – Karnataka announced to get its first Marina.
4. 24 February 2023 – UK overtook India as the world's 6th-biggest stock market with market capitalization of $3.11 trillion.
5. 24 February 2023 – WHO reported that globally, one woman dies every 2 minutes during pregnancy or childbirth (data from 2000-2020).

March 2023

1. 9 March 2023 – India beat Australia 2-1 in the Border-Gavaskar Trophy series; "75 Years of Friendship through Cricket" event in Ahmedabad.
2. 24 March 2023 – MeitY approved setting up of an Electronics Manufacturing Cluster in Dharwad, Karnataka (investment ~Rs 180 crore).
3. 29-30 March 2023 – Ministry of Defence signed contracts worth ~Rs 5,400 crore with BEL and NSIL for equipment to Army and Navy including air defence and satellite systems.
4. 15 March 2023 – The BIS launched "Learning Science via Standards" initiative to improve science education.

5. 15 March 2023 – 13th edition of Exercise Bold Kurukshetra (joint India-Singapore military exercise) concluded at Jodhpur.

April 2023

1. 2 April 2023 – Indian Space Research Organisation (ISRO) successfully conducted the Reusable Launch Vehicle Autonomous Landing Mission (RLV-LEX) at Chitradurga, Karnataka.
2. 6 April 2023 – Indian Air Force participated in multinational exercise *Orion 2023* in France.
3. 8 April 2023 – NASA and ISRO jointly announced the *NISAR* satellite, to be launched in 2024, to study Earth's ecosystems and climate.
4. 13 April 2023 – Prime Minister Modi flagged off India's first semi-high-speed regional rail service *RAPIDX* (Delhi–Meerut corridor trial).
5. 14 April 2023 – The birth anniversary of Dr. B. R. Ambedkar was celebrated nationwide, marking his 132nd Jayanti.
6. 21 April 2023 – India observed *Civil Services Day 2023* in New Delhi.

May 2023

1. 1 May 2023 – International Labour Day observed; discussions focused on India's gig workers' rights.
2. 4 May 2023 – Odisha train collision killed 275+ passengers; one of India's worst rail accidents in decades.
3. 8 May 2023 – Supreme Court of India delivered its verdict on Maharashtra political crisis (Shiv Sena split case).
4. 10 May 2023 – India observed *10th anniversary of National Technology Day*; PM laid foundation of several scientific projects.
5. 14 May 2023 – Karnataka Assembly elections held; Congress won a clear majority.
6. 19 May 2023 – Cyclone Mocha struck the Bay of Bengal region, impacting Myanmar and Bangladesh; India provided relief aid.

June 2023

1. 2 June 2023 – Telangana celebrated its State Formation Day (10th anniversary of bifurcation from Andhra Pradesh).
2. 5 June 2023 – World Environment Day celebrated; theme: *Solutions to Plastic Pollution*.
3. 9 June 2023 – PM Modi inaugurated India's first International Cruise Terminal in Mumbai.

4. 12 June 2023 – World Day Against Child Labour observed; India reviewed its child labour laws.
5. 17 June 2023 – G20 Agriculture Ministers' Meeting held in Hyderabad.
6. 18 June 2023 – 75th International Yoga Day curtain-raiser event held at Jabalpur, Madhya Pradesh.

July 2023

1. 1 July 2023 – National Doctors' Day celebrated; theme focused on medical ethics.
2. 6 July 2023 – India's *Chandrayaan-3* lunar mission successfully launched from Sriharikota.
3. 10 July 2023 – Floods hit several districts of Assam and Bihar; NDRF deployed.
4. 14 July 2023 – Bastille Day parade in Paris; PM Modi attended as Guest of Honour.
5. 18 July 2023 – Monsoon Session of Indian Parliament began.

August 2023

1. 15 August 2023 – 77th Independence Day celebrated; PM Modi addressed the nation from Red Fort.
2. 16 August 2023 – India hosted BRICS Business Forum in Durban, South Africa.
3. 18 August 2023 – Rajya Sabha passed the *Government of National Capital Territory of Delhi (Amendment) Bill 2023*.
4. 21 August 2023 – Chandrayaan-3 entered final lunar orbit for landing preparations.
5. 23 August 2023 – Chandrayaan-3 made a historic soft landing on the Moon's south pole; India became the 4th country to land on the Moon.

September 2023

1. 1 September 2023 – India assumed Chair of Global Partnership on Artificial Intelligence (GPAI).
2. 5 September 2023 – Teachers' Day celebrated across India.
3. 6–10 September 2023 – G20 Leaders' Summit held in New Delhi; African Union admitted as permanent member.
4. 12 September 2023 – India and Saudi Arabia signed major energy cooperation deals.

5. 15 September 2023 – Engineers' Day celebrated (in memory of M. Visvesvaraya).

October 2023

1. 2 October 2023 – Gandhi Jayanti celebrated; Swachh Bharat campaigns held nationwide.
2. 5 October 2023 – Nobel Prizes 2023 announced; Katalin Karikó and Drew Weissman won Medicine Nobel.
3. 11 October 2023 – International Day of the Girl Child observed.
4. 14 October 2023 – India hosted *Global Maritime India Summit 2023.*
5. 20 October 2023 – PM Modi inaugurated India's first Regional Rapid Transit System (RRTS) between Delhi and Meerut.
6. 22 October 2023 – India won ICC Men's Cricket World Cup match against New Zealand at Dharamshala.

November 2023

1. 1 November 2023 – Karnataka, Kerala, MP and other states celebrated *Statehood Day.*
2. 6 November 2023 – Supreme Court reserved judgment in same-sex marriage case.
3. 8 November 2023 – World Radiology Day observed.
4. 12 November 2023 – Diwali celebrated across India.
5. 15 November 2023 – Jharkhand Foundation Day celebrated.
6. 17 November 2023 – India hosted *Global Food Security Summit 2023.*

December 2023

1. 1 December 2023 – World AIDS Day observed; India launched new awareness campaign.
2. 3 December 2023 – International Day of Persons with Disabilities observed.
3. 4 December 2023 – Indian Navy Day celebrated.
4. 9 December 2023 – India signed agreements with UAE on renewable energy cooperation.
5. 10 December 2023 – Human Rights Day observed worldwide.
6. 13 December 2023 – Parliament security breach incident occurred; two intruders jumped into Lok Sabha chamber.

EVENTS IN 2024

January 2024

- 1 January 2024: Brazil assumed the presidency of the G20 for the year 2024, focusing on social inclusion, sustainable development, and food security. President Lula da Silva pledged to bridge global inequality through international cooperation.
- 5 January 2024: A major earthquake of magnitude 7.6 struck western Japan, causing widespread destruction in Ishikawa Prefecture. More than 90 people were reported dead, and thousands were evacuated due to collapsed buildings and tsunami warnings.
- 8 January 2024: The World Health Organization issued an alert about a sharp rise in H5N1 bird flu outbreaks in several Asian and European countries. Health agencies began culling poultry and monitoring human transmissions.
- 10 January 2024: India launched its first solar mission satellite, Aditya-L1, into orbit around the Lagrange Point 1. This mission aims to study solar flares and their impact on Earth's magnetic field and satellite communications.
- 15 January 2024: Heavy snowfall and avalanches disrupted normal life in Jammu & Kashmir, Himachal Pradesh, and Uttarakhand. The Indian Army and Air Force were deployed for rescue operations and airlifting tourists from stranded areas.
- 20 January 2024: Protests erupted in Peru over high inflation and fuel prices, leading to clashes between police and civilians. The government announced emergency financial relief packages and fuel subsidies to calm public anger.

February 2024

- 1 February 2024: The Indian Union Budget 2024-25 was presented by Finance Minister Nirmala Sitharaman. Major allocations focused on infrastructure development, green energy, and support for farmers and women entrepreneurs.
- 5 February 2024: Massive wildfires broke out in central Chile due to high temperatures and strong winds. More than 100 people were reported dead, and thousands of homes were destroyed, leading to a national emergency.

- 10 February 2024: A rare snowfall covered the deserts of Saudi Arabia, especially in the Tabuk region. Locals and tourists captured the unique moment as weather anomalies increased across the Middle East.
- 20 February 2024: A 6.3 magnitude earthquake struck eastern Turkey near the city of Elaz??, injuring hundreds and damaging several buildings. Emergency teams were deployed quickly for rescue and relief operations.
- 26 February 2024: The 2024 ICC Under-19 Cricket World Cup concluded in South Africa, with Australia defeating India in the final. The tournament showcased rising cricket talent from across the globe.

March 2024

- 3 March 2024: NASA and ISRO jointly launched the NISAR satellite to monitor Earth's climate and natural disasters. It became the world's most advanced radar imaging satellite for Earth observation.
- 8 March 2024L International Women's Day was marked with global protests and campaigns demanding gender equality, better representation in leadership roles, and action against gender-based violence.
- 22 March 2024: On World Water Day, the UN warned that over 2 billion people lack safe drinking water. Global leaders pledged more funds to water sustainability programs.

April 2024

- 4 April 2024: NASA named the astronauts for the Artemis II Moon mission, including the first woman and first person of color assigned to a lunar flyby. The mission is scheduled for 2025.
- 10 April 2024: A major dust storm swept across northern India, affecting Delhi, Haryana, and Rajasthan. Flights were delayed and schools were shut due to extremely poor air quality.
- 25 April 2024: India's GDP growth forecast for 2024-25 was raised to 7.2% by the IMF, citing strong manufacturing, digital infrastructure, and domestic demand.

May 2024

- 4 May 2024 : Cyclone Remal hit Bangladesh and West Bengal, bringing heavy rains, flooding, and winds over 100 km/h. Thousands were evacuated as disaster relief teams took charge.

- 9 May 2024 : South Africa held its national elections with record voter turnout. The African National Congress faced a major challenge from opposition parties for the first time in decades.
- 30 May 2024 : Massive forest fires broke out in Alberta, Canada, forcing over 20,000 people to evacuate. Smoke clouds impacted air quality across parts of the U.S. and Europe.

June 2024

- 5 June 2024 : World Environment Day was celebrated with the theme "Land Restoration and Desertification Control." India launched a national program to rejuvenate degraded land.
- 10 June 2024 : The European Union signed a major free trade agreement with ASEAN nations. The deal is expected to boost trade, technology exchange, and climate cooperation.
- 25 June 2024 : France banned disposable vapes as part of a campaign against youth nicotine addiction. The move received praise from health experts worldwide.

July 2024

- 1 July 2024 : India implemented its new education policy in all central schools, emphasizing multilingual learning, coding, and vocational training from an early age.
- 28 July 2024 : Paris hosted the 2024 Summer Olympics opening ceremony at the Seine River, with a floating parade of athletes and high-tech visual displays.

August 2024

- 5 August 2024 : Massive protests erupted in Pakistan against inflation and political arrests. The government imposed emergency law in major cities to maintain order.
- 15 August 2024 : India celebrated its 78th Independence Day with Prime Minister Modi addressing the nation, focusing on self-reliance, AI technology, and green energy goals.
- 30 August 2024 : Hurricane Isaac hit Florida and Georgia with winds over 200 km/h, causing widespread damage. Evacuation orders were issued for over a million people.

September 2024

- 3 September 2024 : China's Chang'e-7 Moon mission successfully landed on the lunar south pole. It marked the country's third soft landing on the Moon, focusing on water ice detection.
- 10 September 2024 : UNESCO added three Indian cultural sites to the World Heritage list, including the ancient Nalanda Mahavihara extension and Majuli Island.
- 17 September 2024 : The United Nations General Assembly opened its 79th session, focusing on climate change, AI governance, and conflict resolution in Gaza and Ukraine.
- 25 September 2024 : Brazil launched a large-scale reforestation project in the Amazon, aiming to restore 5 million hectares of forest by 2030.

October 2024

- 2 October 2024 : Mahatma Gandhi's 155th birth anniversary was observed globally. The Indian government launched a national cleanliness and rural water campaign in his honor.
- 18 October 2024 : Israel and Hamas resumed ceasefire negotiations in Qatar, mediated by the UN. While fragile, the truce held for the first time in months.
- 28 October 2024 : India's Chandrayaan-3 rover completed its lunar surface operations, collecting soil samples and temperature data near the Moon's south pole.

November 2024

- 5 November 2024 : The U.S. Presidential election was held, with Donald Trump defeating Joe Biden in a closely contested vote. Concerns over mail-in ballots sparked minor protests.
- 11 November 2024 : UN climate talks (COP29) began in Dubai, with leaders agreeing to triple renewable energy investments by 2030 and phase out coal gradually.
- 27 November 2024 : Severe drought in Australia led to water rationing in several cities. Farmers demanded federal aid as crop failures hit wheat and cotton production.

December 2024

- 1 December 2024 : Brazil hosted the G20 Leaders' Summit in Rio de

Janeiro, focusing on global inequality, debt relief, and South-South cooperation.

- 18 December 2024 : The FIFA Club World Cup final was held in Saudi Arabia, with Manchester City defeating Flamengo in a high-scoring match.
- 25 December 2024 : Christmas was celebrated globally with a focus on sustainable celebrations. Many churches and communities promoted eco-friendly decorations and low-carbon travel.

EVENT IN 2025

January 2025

- 20 January 2025 : Donald Trump was officially sworn in as the 47th President of the United States for a second non-consecutive term. In his inaugural speech, he emphasized immigration control, energy independence, and renewed ties with traditional allies.
- 25 January 2025 : India celebrated its 76th Republic Day with France's President Emmanuel Macron as the chief guest. The parade showcased India's women-led military contingents and advanced indigenous weapons systems like the Tejas fighter jet.

February 2025

- 4 February 2025 : A mass shooting at a school in Örebro, Sweden, left 11 people dead and over 15 injured, marking the deadliest such incident in Swedish history. The tragedy led to renewed debates on gun control laws in the country.
- 9 February 2025 : Latvia, Lithuania, and Estonia officially disconnected from Russia's electricity grid and joined the European power network, signaling a major energy and political shift in the Baltic region.

March 2025

- 8 March 2025 : On International Women's Day, the Indian government announced a new national scheme offering free education and skill development for girls from rural areas. Global marches were held demanding equal rights and pay for women.
- 21 March 2025 : Severe floods in southern Thailand caused by unexpected torrential rains displaced more than 50,000 people. Emergency relief operations were launched with support from ASEAN neighbors.

April 2025

- 5 April 2025 : NASA's Artemis II mission successfully completed its crewed pre-launch rehearsal. The four-member team, including the first female astronaut to orbit the Moon, is scheduled to launch later in the year.
- 14 April 2025 : Ambedkar Jayanti was celebrated across India with large processions and seminars on social justice. The Prime Minister announced new scholarships for marginalized students in higher education.

May 2025

- 7 May 2025 : India hosted the 18th BRICS Summit in New Delhi. Member countries discussed expanding trade in national currencies and forming a joint fund for green energy research.
- 20 May 2025 : Massive wildfires in southern Spain destroyed over 12,000 hectares of forest. Thousands were evacuated, and firefighting aircraft were deployed as extreme heat worsened the crisis.

June 2025

- 10 June 2025 : The FIFA World Cup 2026 pre-event qualifiers began across Europe and Asia. India played its opening qualifier match against Qatar, drawing national attention and fan enthusiasm.
- 23 June 2025 : The G7 Summit held in Canada focused on Ukraine, AI regulation, and economic revival. Leaders agreed to invest in digital public infrastructure and global cybersecurity cooperation.

July 2025

- 7 July 2025 : A new global heat record was set as temperatures reached 54.4°C in Death Valley, USA. The WHO issued a heat emergency warning, and several countries declared national alerts due to heatstroke-related deaths.
- 14 July 2025 : India launched its first indigenous reusable spaceplane for atmospheric re-entry tests. ISRO hailed the mission as a success and a step toward low-cost satellite launches and future space tourism.

August 2025

- 15 August 2025 - India's 79th Independence Day: India will commemorate its 79th Independence Day with nationwide celebrations, flag hoisting at the Red Fort, and the Prime Minister's address focusing on digital transformation and defence self-reliance.

- 23-29 August 2025 - Rio Climate Action Week (Brazil): A pre-COP30 event held in Rio de Janeiro, bringing together world leaders, scientists and activists to discuss carbon-neutral development and Amazon conservation ahead of the UN climate summit.

September 2025

- 13-21 September 2025 - World Athletics Championships (Tokyo, Japan): The 20th edition of the global athletics meet will showcase elite competition across track and field disciplines, highlighting Japan's sports infrastructure and Asia's growing athletic talent.
- 25 September 2025 - United Nations Sustainable Development Summit (New York, USA): World leaders will gather to assess global progress on the 2030 Agenda for Sustainable Development, with renewed pledges toward poverty reduction and climate action.

October 2025

- 2 October 2025 - International Day of Non-Violence & Gandhi Jayanti (India): Observed globally on Mahatma Gandhi's birth anniversary, the day promotes peace and non-violence. India holds cultural and educational events dedicated to Gandhian ideals.
- 16-18 October 2025 - World Economic Forum Special Meeting (Singapore): Global policymakers and industry leaders will meet to deliberate on economic recovery, artificial intelligence, and sustainable trade policies in the Indo-Pacific region.
- 31 October 2025 – National Unity Day (India): Observed on the birth anniversary of Sardar Vallabhbhai Patel to promote unity, integrity, and national integration.

November 2025

- 10-21 November 2025 - United Nations Climate Change Conference (COP30, Belém, Brazil): A historic climate summit hosted in the Amazon, focusing on biodiversity protection, renewable energy, and implementation of post-Paris climate goals.
- 14 November 2025 – World Diabetes Day: Observed globally to raise awareness about diabetes prevention, treatment, and management.

- 22-23 November 2025 - G20 Leaders' Summit (Johannesburg, South Africa): The 20th G20 summit-first ever held in Africa-will address global economic stability, green growth, and equitable technology access among nations.

December 2025

- 1 December 2025 - World AIDS Day: Observed globally to raise awareness about HIV/AIDS, promote prevention strategies, and support people living with the disease.
- 5 December 2025 – World Soil Day: Celebrated worldwide to highlight the importance of healthy soil for food security, ecosystems, and sustainable development.
- 10 December 2025 - Human Rights Day: Celebrated worldwide to commemorate the adoption of the Universal Declaration of Human Rights and to promote equality, freedom, and justice.
- Mid-December 2025 - United Nations Year-End Review Meetings: The United Nations and its agencies conducted annual review sessions assessing global progress on peace, development, and climate commitments.
- December 2025 - Global Technology and AI Year-End Announcements: Major technology companies and research institutions released reports and announcements highlighting advancements in artificial intelligence, quantum research, and digital innovation.
- 25 December 2025 - Christmas Day: Celebrated worldwide to mark the birth of Jesus Christ, featuring religious observances, cultural celebrations, and social gatherings.

EVENT IN 2026

January 2026

- 1 January 2026 - New Year's Day: The New Year 2026 was celebrated worldwide with cultural events, public gatherings, and resolutions marking the beginning of the year.
- 4 January 2026 - World Braille Day: Observed globally to raise awareness about the importance of Braille as a means of communication for people who are blind or visually impaired.
- Mid-January 2026 - World Economic Forum Annual Meeting (Davos): Global leaders, economists, and industry experts gathered to discuss

international economic trends, climate action, and emerging technologies.

- 15 January 2026 - Indian Army Day (India): Celebrated to commemorate the establishment of the Indian Army, honoring soldiers and their contributions to national security.
- 26 January 2026 - Republic Day (India): India celebrated Republic Day with a grand parade in New Delhi, marking the adoption of the Indian Constitution and showcasing cultural diversity and military strength.

February 2026

- 2 February 2026 - World Wetlands Day: Observed globally to raise awareness about the importance of wetlands for biodiversity, climate regulation, and sustainable development.
- 4 February 2026 - World Cancer Day: Marked worldwide to promote awareness, prevention, detection, and treatment of cancer.
- 11 February 2026 - International Day of Women and Girls in Science: Celebrated to encourage equal access and participation of women in science and technology fields.
- 14 February 2026 - Valentine's Day: Celebrated in many countries as a day dedicated to love, relationships, and social bonding.
- 20 February 2026 - World Day of Social Justice: Observed to promote social equity, inclusion, human rights, and fair opportunities for all.
- 21 February 2026 - International Mother Language Day: Celebrated to promote linguistic diversity, multilingual education, and preservation of cultural heritage.
- 27 February 2026 - World NGO Day: Recognizes and honors the contributions of non-governmental organizations in social development, humanitarian work, and global progress.

❑❑❑